The Order of Books

The Order of Books

Readers, Authors, and Libraries
in Europe between the
Fourteenth and Eighteenth Centuries

Roger Chartier

Translated by Lydia G. Cochrane

Stanford University Press
Stanford, California
1994

Stanford University Press
Stanford, California
© 1992 Editions Alinea
English translation © 1994 Polity Press
Originally published 1992 in France as *L'ordre des livres*
    by Editions Alinea
Originating publisher of English edition: Polity Press,
    Cambridge, in association with Blackwell Publishers
First published in the U.S.A. by Stanford University Press
Printed in Great Britain
Cloth ISBN 0-8047-2266-8
Paper ISBN 0-8047-2267-6
LC 93-84986

Printed with the assistance of the French Ministry
    of Culture

This book is printed on acid-free paper

Contents

Preface

In bringing together under this title the three essays that make up this book I hope to highlight a question that runs all through it: how did people in Western Europe between the end of the Middle Ages and the eighteenth century attempt to master the enormously increased number of texts that first the manuscript book and then print put into circulation? Inventorying titles, categorizing works, and attributing texts were all operations that made it possible to set the world of the written word in order. Our own age is the direct heir of this immense effort motivated by anxiety. It was in those decisive centuries, when the hand-copied book was gradually replaced by works composed in movable type and printed on presses, that the acts and thoughts that are still our own were forged. The invention of the author as the fundamental principle for the designation of a text, the dream of a universal library, real or imaginary, containing all the works that have ever been wirtten, and the emergence of a new definition of the book that made an indissoluble connection between an object, a text, and an author – these are some of the innovations that transformed people's relationship with texts, both before and after Gutenberg.

That relationship typically contains an internal contradiction. On the one hand, every reader has to deal with an entire set of constraints and obligations. The author, the bookseller-publisher, the commentator, and the censor all have an interest in keeping close control over the production of meaning and in making sure that the text that they have written, published, glossed, or authorized will be understood with no possible deviation from their prescriptive will. On the other hand, reading, by definition, is rebellious and vagabond. Readers use infinite numbers of subterfuges to procure prohibited books, to read between the lines, and to subvert the lessons imposed on them.

The book always aims at installing an order, whether it is the order in which it is deciphered, the order in which it is to be understood, or the order intended by the authority who commanded or permitted the work. This multifaceted order is not all-powerful, however, when it comes to annulling the reader's liberty. Even when it is hemmed in by differences in competence and by conventions, liberty knows how to distort and reformulate the significations that were supposed to defeat it. The dialectic between imposition and appropriation, between constraints transgressed and freedoms bridled, is not the same in all places or all times or for all people. Recognizing its diverse modalities and multiple variations is the first aim of a history of reading that strives to grasp – in all their differences – communities of readers and their 'arts of reading'.

The order of books has still another meaning. Whether they are in manuscript or in print, books are objects whose forms, if they cannot impose the sense of the texts that they bear, at least command the uses that can invest them and the appropriations to which they are susceptible. Works and discourses exist only when they become physical realities and are inscribed on the pages of a book, transmitted by a voice reading or narrating, or spoken on the stage of a theatre. Understanding the principles that govern the 'order of discourse' supposes that the principles underlying the processes of production, communication, and reception of books (and other objects that bear writing) will also be deciphered in a rigorous manner. More than even before, historians of literary works and historians of cultural practices have become aware of the effects of meaning that material forms produce. In the case of the book, those forms constitute a singular order totally distinct from other registers of transmission of the canonical works as ordinary texts. This means that, even though it is not emphasized in the present book, keen attention should be paid to the technical, visual, and physical devices that organize the reading of writing when writing becomes a book.

This work has another aim in its three chapters: to initiate more general reflection on the reciprocal relations between the two meanings that we spontaneously give to the term 'culture'. The first designates the works and the acts that lend themselves to aesthetic or intellectual appreciation in any given society; the second aims at ordinary, banal practices that express the way in which a community – on any scale – experiences and conceives of its relationship with the world, with others, and with itself.

Works – even the greatest works, especially the greatest works – have no stable, universal, fixed meaning. They are invested with plural and mobile significations that are constructed in the encounter between a proposal and a reception. The meanings attributed to their forms and their themes depend upon the areas of competence or the expectations of the various publics that take hold of them. To be sure, the creators (or the 'powers' or the 'clerics') always aspire to pin down their meaning and proclaim the correct interpretation, the interpretation that ought to constrain reading (or viewing). But without fail reception invents, shifts about, distorts.

Works are produced within a specific order that has its own rules, conventions, and hierarchies, but they escape all these and take on a certain density in their peregrinations – which can be in a very long time span – about the social world. Deciphered on the basis of mental and affective schemes that constitute the 'culture' (in the anthropological sense) of the communities that receive them, works turn the tables and become a precious resource for thinking about what is essential: the construction of social ties, individual subjectivity, and relationship with the sacred.

Conversely, any work inscribes within its forms and its themes a relationship with the manner in which, in a given moment and place, modes of exercising power, social configurations, or the structure of personality are organized. Thought of (and thinking of himself or herself) as a demiurge, the writer none the less creates in a state of dependence. Dependence upon the rules (of patronage, subsidy, and the market) that define the writer's condition. Dependence (on an even deeper level) on the unconscious determinations that inhabit the work and that make it conceivable, communicable, and decipherable.

To consider in this way that all works are anchored in the practices and the institutions of the social world is not to postulate any general equivalence among all the products of the mind. Some, better than others, never exhaust their significative force. If we try to understand this by invoking the universality of beauty or the unity of human nature we will fall short of the truth. The essential game is being played elsewhere, in the complex, subtle, shifting relationships established between the forms (symbolic or material) proper to works, which are unequally open to appropriation, and the habits or the concerns of the various publics for those works.

What any cultural history must take into consideration today is the paradoxical articulation between a *difference* – the difference by means of which all societies, with varying modalities, have separated out from daily practice a particlar domain of human activity – and *dependencies* – the dependencies that take a variety of ways to inscribe aesthetic and intellectual invention within the conditions of possibility and intelligibility. This problematic connection is rooted in the very trajectory that gives works their most powerful meanings – meanings constructed on the aesthetic or reflective transfiguration of ordinary experiences, grasped on the basis of practices proper to those works' various publics.

Reflection on how the figure of the author was constructed, on the rules for the formation of communities of readers, or on the significance invested in the building of libraries (with or without walls) may perhaps contribute to focusing a few of the questions that currently inhabit the disciplines of knowledge and public debate. By reintroducing variation and difference where the illusion of universality spontaneously springs up, such reflection may help us to get rid of some of our over-sure distinctions and some over-familiar truisms.

1

Communities of Readers

Far from being writers – founders of their own place, heirs of the peasants of earlier ages now working on the soil of language, diggers of wells and builders of houses – readers are travellers; they move across lands belonging to someone else, like nomads poaching their way across fields they did not write, despoiling the wealth of Egypt to enjoy it themselves. Writing accumulates, stocks up, resists time by the establishment of a place and multiplies its production through the expansionism of reproduction. Reading takes no measures against the erosion of time (one forgets oneself and also forgets), it does not keep what it acquires, or it does so poorly, and each of the places through which it passes is a repetition of the lost paradise.[1]

This magnificent passage from Michel de Certeau which contrasts writing – conservative, fixed, durable – and reading – always of the order of the ephemeral – constitutes both an obligatory base and a disquieting challenge for any history that hopes to inventory and make sense out of a practice (reading) that only rarely leaves traces, that is scattered in an infinity of singular acts, and that easily shakes off all constraints. Such a proposal is based on a dual presupposition: that reading is not already inscribed in the text with no conceivable gap between the meaning assigned to it (by its author, by custom, by criticism, and so forth) and the interpretation that its readers might make of it; and, as a corollary, that a text exists only because there is a reader to give it meaning. To return to Michel de Certeau:

> Whether it is a question of newspapers or Proust, the text has a meaning only through its readers; it changes along with them; it is ordered in accord with codes of perception that it does not control. It becomes a text only in its relation to the exteriority of the reader, by an interplay of implications and ruses between two sorts of 'expectation' in combination: the expectation that organizes a *readable* space (a literality), and one that organizes a procedure necessary for the *actualization* of the work (a reading).[2]

The historian's task is thus to reconstruct the variations that differentiate the *espaces lisibles* – that is, the texts in their discursive and material forms – and those that govern the circumstances of their *effectuation* – that is, the readings, understood as concrete practices and as procedures of interpretation.

Michel de Certeau's suggestions provide a basis for suggesting some of what is at stake and the problems and conditions of possibility of this sort of history. Its space is usually defined by three poles that the academic tradition usually keeps separate: first, the analysis of texts, be they canonical or ordinary, to discern their structures, their themes, and their aims; second, the history of books and, beyond that, the history of all objects and all forms that bear texts; third, the study of practices that seize on these objects and these forms in a variety of ways and produce differentiated uses and meanings. For me, a fundamental question underlies this approach that combines textual criticism, bibliography, and cultural history: in the societies of the ancien régime, how did increased circulation of printed matter transform forms of sociability, permit new modes of thought, and change people's relationship with power?

Hence the need to stress the way in which the encounter between 'the world of the text' and 'the world of the reader' – to use Paul Ricoeur's terms – operates.[3] To reconstruct this process of the 'actualization' of texts in its historical dimensions first requires that we accept the notion that their meanings are dependent upon the forms through which they are received and appropriated by their readers (or hearers). Readers and hearers, in point of fact, are never confronted with abstract or ideal texts detached from all materiality; they manipulate or perceive objects and forms whose structures and modalities govern their reading (or their hearing), thus the possible comprehension of the text read (or heard). Against a purely semantic definition of the text (which inhabits not only structuralist criticism in all its variants but also the literary theories most attuned to a reconstruction of the reception of works), one must state that forms produce meaning and that a text, stable in its letter, is invested with a new meaning and status when the mechanisms that make it available to interpretation change.

We must also keep in mind that reading is always a practice embodied in acts, spaces, and habits. Far from being a phenomenology that wipes out all concrete modalities of the act of reading and characterizes that act by its effects, which are postulated to be universal (as with the operation of response to the text that makes the subject better understand himself or herself thanks to the mediation of interpretation), a history of reading must identify the specific mechanisms that distinguish the various communities of readers and traditions of reading. This move supposes the recognition of several sets of contrasts, the first of which is in the realm of reading ability. The essential but oversimplified separation of the literate from the illiterate does not exhaust the full range of differences in the reader's relation to writing. All who can read texts do not read them in the same fashion, and there is an enormous gap between the virtuosi among readers and the least skilled at reading, who have to oralize what they are reading in order to comprehend it and who are at ease only with a limited range of textual or typographical forms. There are equally great differences between the norms and conventions of reading that define, for each community of readers, legitimate uses of the book, ways to read, and the instruments and methods of interpretations. Finally, there are differences between the expectations and interests that various groups of readers invest in the practice of reading. Such expectations and interests, which govern practices, determine the way in which texts can be read and read differently by readers who do not have the same intellectual baggage or the same relationship with the written word.

Michel de Certeau gives an illustration of this sort of approach when he discusses the characteristics of mystical reading: 'By "mystical readings" I mean the set of reading procedures advised or practiced in the field of experience of the solitaries or the collectives designated in the sixteenth and seventeenth centuries as "illuminated," "mystic" or "spiritual".'[4] In this minor, marginal, and dispersed community that was the mystical milieu, reading was regulated by norms and habits that invested the book with original functions: it replaced the institution of the church, held to be insufficient; it made discourse possible (the discourse of prayer, of communication with God, of the *conversar*); it indicated the practices by which spiritual experience could be constructed. The mystical relationship with the book can also be understood as a trajectory in which several 'moments' of reading succeed one another: the installation of an alterity that provides a basis for the subjective quest, the unfolding of a sense of joy, a physical reaction to the 'manducation' of the text that leaves its mark on the body, and, at the end of the process, cessation of reading, abandonment of the book, and absolute detachment. One of the first tasks of a history of reading that hopes to understand the varieties of the paradigmatic figure of the reader as poacher is thus to ascertain the networks of reading practices and the rules for reading proper to the various communities of readers – spiritual, intellectual, professional, and so forth.[5]

But to read is always to read something. Naturally, if it is to exist the history of reading must be radically distinguished from a history of what is read: 'The reader emerges from the history of the book, in which he has long been merged, indistinct. . . . The reader was taken to be the effect of the book. Today he becomes detached from those books whose mere shadow he was supposed to be. And now that shadow is unshackled, it takes on relief and acquires an independence.'[6] That founding independence is not an arbitrary liberty. It is limited by the codes and the conventions that regulate the practices of a membership community. It is also limited by the discursive and material forms of the texts read.

'New readers make new texts and their new meanings are a function of their new forms.'[7] D. F. McKenzie perspicaciously notes here the dual set of variations – variations in the readers' resources and in textual and formal mechanisms – that any history that takes on the task of restoring the fluid and plural signification of texts must take into account. One can profit from McKenzie's dictum in several ways: by noting the major oppositions that distinguish the various modes of reading from one another; by specifying the practices most popular among readers; by focusing attention on the publishing formulas that offer old texts to new readers of a humbler sort and in greater number.

This perspective reflects a dual dissatisfaction with the history of the book in France in the last twenty or thirty years, where the historians' chief concern has been to measure the unequal presence of the book in the various groups that made up the society of the ancien régime. This led to the construction (incidentally, quite necessarily so) of indicators to reveal cultural gaps at a given place and time: among such indicators are the percentage of probate inventories mentioning ownership of books, the classification of book collections according to the number of works they included, and thematic description of private libraries according to the place that the various bibliographical categories occupy in them. In this perspective, giving an account of the reading matter of the French between the sixteenth and the eighteenth century was above all a question of constructing data sets, establishing quantitative thresholds, and noting the cultural equivalents of social differences.

These procedures were adopted collectively (by the author of the present work among others), and they permitted the accumulation of a body of knowledge without which further investigation would have been inconceivable. They raise problems, however. First, such procedures rest on a narrowly sociographic conception implicitly postulating that cultural cleavages are necessarily organized according to pre-existent social divisions. I think we need to reject this dependence that relates gaps in cultural practices to a priori social oppositions, whether on the macroscopic scale of contrasts between dominant and dominated or between the elites and the people or on the scale of smaller differentiations, as for example among social groups in a hierarchy of conditions, professions, or levels of wealth.

Cultural divisions are not obligatorily organized in accordance with the one grid of social divisions that supposedly commands the unequal presence of objects or differences in behaviour patterns. We must turn the perspective around and begin by designating the social areas in which each corpus of texts and each genre of printed matter circulates. Beginning with objects, in this fashion, rather than with classes or groups leads to considering that the French style of sociocultural history has too long continued to exist on the basis of a mutilated conception of the social. By privileging only socioprofessional classification it has forgotten that other and equally social principles of differentiation might explain cultural divisions even more pertinently. The same is true of gender-based and generationally based distinctions, of religious affiliations, of communitarian solidarities, of educative or corporative traditions, and more.

Furthermore, the history of the book in its social and quantitative definition attempted to characterize cultural configurations on the basis of the categories of texts that were supposed to be specific to those configurations. This operation was doubly reductive. First, it equated the identification of differences with mere inequalities in distribution; second, it ignored the process by which a text takes on meaning for those who read it. Several shifts of emphasis could be proposed to correct these postulates. The first situates the recognition of the differences most deeply rooted in society in differing uses of shared materials. In the societies of the ancien régime the *same* texts were appropriated by 'popular' readers and other readers more than has been thought. Either readers of more humble social condition were put in possession of books that were not specifically designed for them (as was the case of Menocchio, the Friuli miller, Jamerey Duval, the shepherd from Lorraine, or Ménétra, the Paris glazier),[8] or else inventive and canny bookseller-printers made available to a very large clientele texts that formerly had circulated only in the narrow world of wealth and letters (which was the case with the *pliegos sueltos* of Castile and the Catalan *plecs*, English chapbooks or the publishing formula known in France under the generic title of the Bibliothèque bleue). What is essential is thus to understand how the same texts can be differently apprehended, manipulated, and comprehended.

A second shift of emphasis reconstructs the networks of practices that organized historically and socially differentiated modes of access of texts. Reading is not uniquely an abstract operation of the intellect: it brings the body into play, it is inscribed in a space and a relationship with oneself or with others. This is why special attention should be paid to ways of reading that have disappeared in our contemporary world. One of these is reading aloud in its dual function of communicating the written word to those who are unable to decipher it themselves but also of cementing the interlocking forms of sociability that are emblematic of private life in the intimacy of the family circle, in worldly conviviality, and in literary circles and spheres of scholarly sociability. A history of reading must not limit itself to the genealogy of our own contemporary manner of reading, in silence and using only our eyes; it must also (and perhaps above all) take on the task of retracing forgotten gestures and habits that have not existed for some time. The challenge matters because it reveals not only the distant foreignness of practices that were common long ago but also the specific structure of texts composed for uses that are not the uses of today's readers of those same texts. In the sixteenth and seventeenth centuries the reading style implicit in a text, literary or not, was still often an oralization of the text, and the 'reader' was an implicit auditor of a read discourse. The work, which was addressed to the ear as much as to the eye, plays with forms and procedures that subject writing to demands more appropriate to oral 'performance'. Many examples of this sort of continuing link between the text and the human voice can be found, from the motifs in *Don Quixote* to the structure of texts adapted for the Bibliothèque bleue.[9]

'Whatever they may do, authors do not write books. Books are not written at all. They are manufactured by scribes and other artisans, by mechanics and other engineers, and by printing presses and other machines.'[10] This remark can serve to introduce the third shift in emphasis that I would like to suggest. Contrary to representation elaborated by literature itself and taken up by the most quantitative form of history of the book, which state that the text exists in and of itself, separate from anything material, we need to remember that there is no text apart from the physical support that offers it for reading (or hearing), hence there is no comprehension of any written piece that does not at least in part depend upon the forms in which it reaches its reader. This means that we need to make a distinction between two sets of mechanisms, the ones that are part of the strategies of writing and the author's intentions, and the ones that result from publishing decisions or the constraints of the print shop.

9

True, authors do not write books: they write texts that become written objects, which may be hand-written, engraved, or printed (and, today, electronically reproduced and transmitted). The space between text and object, which is precisely the space in which meaning is constructed, has too often been forgotten, not only by the traditional sort of literary history that thinks of the work as an abstract text whose typographic forms are without importance, but also by the 'aesthetic of reception' that, in spite of its desire to historicize the readers' experience, postulates a pure and unmediated relationship between the 'signals' emitted by the text (which play with accepted literary conventions) and the 'horizon of expectation' of the public to which those signals are addressed. In this perspective the 'effect produced' in no way depends upon the material forms that operate as a vehicle for the text.[11] Still, those forms also fully contribute to fashioning the reader's expectations and to calling for a new public or novel uses.

Thus we have been brought back to the triangle that was our point of departure, the relationship set up among the text, the book, and the reader. The variations in that relationship describe several simple figures for the connection between 'readable space' (*espace lisible*) and 'effectuation', to use Michel de Certeau's terms. The first variation considers a stable, literal text that is available for reading in printed forms that change. In his study of the innovations introduced into editions of William Congreve's plays at the beginning of the eighteenth century, D. F. McKenzie has shown how apparently insignificant formal changes (moving from a quarto to an octavo edition, numbering scenes, the presence or absence of a decorative element printed between one scene and the next, recalling the names of characters present at the

beginning of each scene, marginal indications of the name
of the character speaking, mention of exits and entrances)
had an important effect on the status of the works. A new
readability was created by a format that was easier to
manipulate and by a page layout that reproduced within
the book something of the movement of the staging, thus
breaking with time-honoured conventions that required
plays to be printed with no restitution of their theatrical
character. This was thus a new manner of reading the
same text, but it also provided a new horizon of reception
because the mechanisms used in the octavo edition of
1710, borrowed from devices used for printed editions of
French plays, gave a new legitimacy to Congreve's plays,
henceforth 'classics' and part of the literary canon, and
induced their author to make changes here and there to
refine the style of his works and make them conform
better to their new 'typographic' dignity.[12] Variations in
the most purely formal aspects of a text's presentation can
thus modify both its register of reference and its mode of
interpretation.

The same is true, on a greater scale, of the greatest
change in the way texts were cast into print between the
sixteenth and the eighteenth centuries, 'the definitive
triumph of white over black'[13] – that is, the introduction
of breathing space on to the page by the use of more
paragraphs to break up an uninterrupted continuous text
and by paragraph indentations that make the order of
discourse immediately visible. The new publishers suggested a new reading of the same texts or the same genres,
a reading that fragmented the text into separate units and
echoed the intellectual or discursive articulation of the
argument in the visual articulation of the page.

Chopping up the text in this manner could have far-
reaching implications where Scripture was concerned.

John Locke was troubled by the new custom of dividing the text of the Bible into chapter and verse. For him it risked obliterating the powerful coherence of the Word of God. Locke says, speaking of the Epistles of Paul, 'Not only the Common People take the Verses usually for distinct Aphorisms, but even Men of more advanc'd Knowledge in reading them, lose very much of the strength and force of the Coherence and the Light that depends on it.' The effects of breaking up Scripture in this manner were disastrous: it authorized every religious sect or party to found its legitimacy on the scriptural passages that seemed to support its views:

> If a Bible was printed as it should be, and as the several Parts of it were writ, in continued Discourses where the Argument is continued, I doubt not that the several Parties would complain of it, as an Innovation, and a dangerous Change in the publishing of those holy Books. . . . He [the member of a particular church] need but be furnished with Verses of Sacred Scriptures, containing Words and Expressions that are but flexible . . . and his System that has appropriated them to the Orthodoxie of his Church, makes them immediately strong and irrefragable Arguments for his Opinion. This is the Benefit of loose Sentences, and Scripture crumbled into Verses, which quickly turn into independent Aphorisms.[14]

A second figure pertains when a text is transferred from one form of publishing to another, dictating both a transformation of the text and the constitution of a new public. This is quite obviously the case with the corpus of titles that made up the catalogue of the Bibliothèque bleue. If that series has long claimed the attention of French historians it is because it has seemed to furnish direct access to the 'popular culture' of the ancien régime, which has been supposed to have been expressed and nourished by works such as these and distributed en masse among the humbler sort of readers.[15] This was not really the case, and for three main reasons. First, it is clear that the works that made up the French stock of the pedlar's book trade had never been written for that purpose. The Bibliothèque bleue was a publishing formula that dipped into the repertory of already published texts and picked out the ones that seemed most likely to meet the expectations of the broad public it sought to reach. Thus we need to take two precautions: not to take texts in the familiar blue format as 'popular' in and of themselves because they belonged to all the genres of learned literature; to keep in mind that such texts usually had an earlier publishing existence and often a long publishing history before they entered the repertory of books for a wide audience.

A study of the works in the 'popular' catalogue has shown that techniques of the most formal and material kind can by themselves inscribe indications of cultural differentiation in published works. In fact, the basic specificity of the Bibliothèque bleue resided in editorial changes made in the texts in order to make them readable by the wide clientele that the publishers were aiming at. The vast labour of adaptation – shortening texts, simplifying them, cutting them up, providing illustrations – was commanded by how the bookseller-publishers who specialized in that market envisioned their customers' abilities and expectations. Thus the very structure of their books was governed by the way that book publishers thought that their target clientele read.

That reading style was always thought to demand such visible signals as anticipatory headings, recapitulative summaries, or woodcuts that functioned as reading protocols much like the mansions in the system of the arts of memory – a style of reading at ease only with brief and self-enclosed sequences set off from one another and readers content with a minimal level of coherence. It was certainly not the manner of reading typical of the lettered elites of the age, even if certain notables deigned to buy the blue-covered books. Works printed for a broad public counted on their readers' previous knowledge. By the recurrence of extremely coded forms, by the repetition of motifs that return from one work to another, and by reuse of the same illustrations, an acquaintance with texts that the reader had already encountered was mobilized into serving for the comprehension of unfamiliar reading matter. In this way the 'blue' catalogue organized a manner of reading that was more recognition than true discovery. It is thus specific formal aspects of the 'blue' editions and the modifications that they imposed on the works they made use of that reveal their 'popular' character.

In proposing this re-evaluation of the Bibliothèque bleue my intention has not been uniquely to reach a better understanding of the most powerful of the instruments of acculturation to the written culture in ancien régime France.[16] It has also been to say that identification of sociocultural differentiations and a study of formal and material mechanisms, far from being mutually exclusive, are necessarily connected. This is so not only because forms are modelled on the expectations and abilities attributed to the public at which they are aimed, but above all because works and objects produce their social area of reception much more than they are produced by crystallized and previously existent divisions. Lawrence W. Levine has proposed a fine demonstration of this.[17] Analyzing the way in which Shakespeare's plays were produced in America (mixed in with other genres such as melodrama, farce, circus turns, dance, and so forth), Levine shows how this type of representation created a numerous public that was 'popular' in that it was not limited to the lettered elite and that it participated actively in the performance by its emotions and reactions. In the late nineteenth century the strict division that was established among genres, styles, and places split up this 'general' public, reserving Shakespeare to the 'legitimate' theatre and a smaller audience and sending off the rest of the audience to more 'popular' entertainments. Changes in the actual form in which Shakespeare's plays were presented (but the same was true of symphonic music, the opera, and works of art) played a large part in the constitution of a 'cultural bifurcation', and a time of mixed and shared offerings was succeeded by a time in which a process of cultural distinction produced a social separation. The traditional mechanisms for representing the Shakespearian repertory in America were thus of the same order as the 'typographic' transformations that the publishers of the Bibliothèque bleue performed on the works they chose: in both cases, the intent was to inscribe the text into a cultural matrix that was not the one that its original creators had in mind, and by that means to permit 'readings', comprehensions, and uses that might have been disqualified by other intellectual habits.

These two examples lead us to consider cultural gaps as the effect of dynamic processes rather than as an expression of static and fixed divisions. On the one hand, a transformation in the forms and the mechanisms through which a text is proposed authorized new appropriations, thus it created new publics and new uses. On the other hand, the fact that an entire society shared the same objects invited a search for new differences to mark distances that had been maintained. The trajectory of print works in ancien régime France stands as witness to this. It was as if the distinctions among ways to read were progressively reinforced as printed matter became less rare, less often confiscated, and a more ordinary commodity. Whereas the mere possession of a book had long signified cultural difference, with the conquests of printing, reading postures and typographical objects were gradually invested with that function. Henceforth readers of distinction and handsome books stood opposed to hastily printed works and their awkward decipherers.

As we have seen, however, both groups often read the same texts, whose plural and contradictory significations were invented along with their varying uses. This means that the question becomes one of selection: why did certain texts lend themselves better than others to durable and multiple reuse?[18] Or at least why did book publishers consider them capable of reaching very different publics? The response lies in the subtle relationships that were set up between the structure of the works, which were not all open to reappropriation in the same degree, and the multiple determinations, both institutional and formal, that regulated their possible 'application' (in the hermeneutic sense of the term) to very different historical situations.

There is a third figure of the relationship among text, print, and reading when a text that is stable in its letter and fixed in its form is apprehended by new readers who read it in other ways than did previous readers. 'A book changes by the fact that it does not change when the world changes'[19] or, to change the statement to fit the scope of the present work, '. . . when its mode of reading changes'. This remark is enough to justify a projected history of reading practices that would seek to identify the major oppositions that can give different meanings to a *same* text. It is perhaps time to question three of these fundamental cleavages, which are held to be certain. First, the opposition between a reading in which comprehension depends upon oralization, either out loud or mumbled, and another, possibly visual, reading.[20] Even though his chronology is open to question, let me recall Michel de Certeau's remark about the reader's freedom and silent reading:

> Reading has become, over the past three centuries, a visual poem. It is no longer accompanied, as it used to be, by the murmur of a vocal articulation or by the movement of a muscular manducation. To read without uttering the words aloud or at least mumbling them is a 'modern' experience, unknown for millennia. In earlier times, the reader interiorized the text; he made his voice the body of the other; he was its actor. Today, the text no longer imposes its own rhythm on the subject, it no longer manifests itself through the reader's voice. This withdrawal of the body, which is the condition of autonomy, is a distancing of the text. It is the reader's *habeas corpus*.[21]

The second accepted cleavage falls between an 'intensive', reverential, and respectful reading of a small number of books that relies on hearing and memory and an 'extensive' reading that consumes many texts, passes nonchalantly from one text to the next, and holds less sacred what is read.[22] The third cleavage is between a private, cloistered, solitary reading, considered to be one of the essential elements for constituting a sphere of private life, and the collective reading – both disciplined and rebellious – of communitarian spaces.[23]

These widely accepted oppositions suggest a chronology that sees as major mutations the gradual advances in silent reading in the Middle Ages and the entry into the world of extensive reading in the late eighteenth century. They prompt several reflections, however: some of these would reduce the simplicity of the dichotomies present in these contrasts by shifting attention to gradations within each opposed entity, by introducing nuances into the criteria that too abruptly differentiate styles of reading, and by reversing the automatic association of the collective with the popular and the elite with the private.[24] Others suggest a connection among three sets of transformations whose effects have often been imperfectly untangled: 'revolutions' that have taken place in techniques for the reproduction of texts (first among them, a shift from 'scribal culture' to 'print culture'); changes in the very forms of the book (the change from the roll or *volumen* to the book in signatures or *codex* during the early centuries of the Christian era was the most fundamental of these but other and less sweeping changes modified the visual aspect of the printed page between the sixteenth and eighteenth century);[25] wide-scale change in reading skills and in modes of reading. These different evolutions did not develop at the same pace and were not punctuated by the same breaking-points. The most interesting question posed to and by the history of reading today is certainly that of the ways in which these three sets of mutations – technological, formal, and cultural – related to one another.

The response to that question obviously depends upon a re-evaluation of the trajectories and divisions characteristic of the society of the ancien régime. More than is admitted, they were organized on the basis of the presence of written matter. That presence has long been gauged uniquely in one of two ways: either by signature counts aimed at establishing literacy rates, hence at evaluating variations in the ability to read according to ages, sites, sexes, and conditions; or by scrutiny of library inventories drawn up by notaries or booksellers in an attempt to measure the circulation of books and reading traditions.

In societies of the ancien régime as in our own, however, access to print cannot be reduced to book ownership alone: every book that is read is not necessarily a book that is personally owned, and all printed matter kept in the home is not obligatorily a book. Moreover, written materials lay at the very heart of the culture of the illiterate and were present in rituals, public spaces, and the work place.[26] Thanks to speech, which deciphered writing, and to the image, which mirrored it, written matter was made accessible even to those who were incapable of reading it or who, left to their own devices, would have had only a rudimentary comprehension of it. Literacy rates do not give an accurate measure of familiarity with the written word – all the more so since in older societies, where learning to read and learning to write were two separate and successive operations, there were many individuals (women in particular) who left school knowing how to read at least a little but not how to write.[27] Similarly, individual possession of a book is an inadequate indication of how often those who were too poor to have any sort of 'library' in their homes might have handled a printed text.

Even if it is totally impossible to establish the number of readers who were not even able to sign their names or the number of readers who owned no books (or at least no books worthy of being appraised by the notary who drew up the inventory) but who could read signs and posters, news-sheets and chapbooks, we none the less have to postulate that they were many in order to comprehend the impact of printed written matter on the older forms of

19

a culture that was still largely oral, action-based, and icono-graphic. The two modes of expression and communication dovetailed in many ways. To take first the ways in which writing and gesture mixed: not only was the written word at the centre of urban festivities such as religious ceremonies, but a number of texts were intended to cancel themselves out as discourse and to produce practical results in behaviour recognized as being in conformity with social or religious norms. This was the case with the civility books, which aimed at teaching the rules of polite social intercourse or Christian propriety.[28]

There was also a dovetailing of speech and writing, which operated in two ways: first, the texts destined by their author and (more often) by their publisher to the most popular public often contained formulas or themes that came directly from the culture of the tale and oral recitation. The writing style of certain *occasionnels* (news-sheets) that imitate the speech patterns of tale-tellers and the variants introduced in the 'blue' editions of fairy tales (which all originally came from literary collections) are good examples of an orality coming to the surface in printed matter.[29] Second, as we have seen, a number of 'readers' apprehended texts only thanks to the mediation of a voice reading them. Comprehending the specificity of this relationship with the written word thus supposes that not all reading must necessarily be individual, solitary, and silent, but, quite to the contrary, that one must acknowledge the importance and the diversity of reading aloud, a practice that has largely been lost.

This acknowledgement, which points to the strength of the penetration of print culture in ancien régime societies, leads to several others. First, it can account for the importance given to written matter and to the objects that bore writing by all the authorities who intended to regulate behaviour and fashion minds. Hence the pedagogical, acculturating, and disciplining role attributed to the texts put into circulation for a wide readership; hence also the controls exercised over printed matter, which was subjected to censorship to eliminate anything that might threaten religious or moral order. Michel de Certeau invited us to recognize both the efficacy of these constraints, which were more and more binding as the individual was more strongly connected with the institution that decreed them ('The creativity of the reader grows as the institution that controlled it declines'),[30] and the various modalities for bridling the reader's interpretation, which ranged from exterior censorship – administrative, judiciary, inquisitorial, scholastic, and so forth – to constraining mechanisms within the book itself.

Texts from bygone years construct representations of the possible uses of the written word and the various ways of handling printed matter in which we can recognize the cleavages that those who produced books held to be decisive. Such perceptions are essential to the extent that they underlie strategies for writing and for publishing that were governed by the supposed skills and expectations of the various target publics. Hence those perceptions acquire an efficacy traces of which can be found in explicit protocols for reading, in the forms given to typographical objects, or in the transformations that changed a text when it was given to new readers in a new publishing formula. It is thus on the basis of the various representations of reading and of the dichotomies constructed in the early modern age (between the reading of a text and the reading of an image; between literate reading and hesitant reading; between intimate reading and communitarian reading) that we must attempt to understand the uses of and adjustments made in these print pieces humbler than the book but just as omnipresent and which ranged from *images volantes* (illustrated broadsheets) and *placards* (topical illustrations and commentary) to the *occasionnels* and the little blue books (which often had illustrations).

Representations of older forms of reading and of the differences among them, as they are revealed on the practical level by the process of casting a text into printed form, or representations of their normative purposes in literary, pictorial, and autobiographical works constitute the basic data for an archaeology of reading practices. None the less, although they express the contrasts that were uppermost in the minds of their contemporaries, they mask other and less clearly perceived cleavages. For example, it is certain that many practices reversed the very terms of the opposition that has so often been depicted between solitary reading in the privacy of a bourgeois or aristocratic setting and reading in common among popular listeners. In reality, reading aloud while others listened long remained one of the practices that cemented elite sociability; conversely, printed matter penetrated to the very heart of the humble home, where it imbued modest objects that were by no means always books with traces of an important moment in private life, a memory of an emotion, or a sign of identity. Contrary to the classical image of 'the people', a product of the early modern age, 'the people' is not always to be sought in the plural, but rather in the secret solitude of the humble practices of individuals who cut out the images of the *occasionnels*, who coloured printed engravings, and who read the chapbooks for simple enjoyment.

The approach proposed in the present work (and put into effect in a few others) is tied to a particular terrain (France between the sixteenth and the eighteenth century) and to a specific problem (the effects of the penetration of printed written matter on the culture of the greater number). It attempts to put into operation two propositions of Michel de Certeau. The first recalls, against all reductive attempts to deny the creative and inventive force of practice, that reading is never totally constraint and that it cannot be deduced from the texts it makes use of. The second stresses that readers' tactics, insinuated in the *lieu propre* (place of their own) produced by the strategies of writing, obey rules, follow logical systems, and imitate models. This reflects the paradox underlying any history of reading, which is that it must postulate the liberty of a practice that it can only grasp, massively, in its determinations. Constructing communities of readers as 'interpretive communities' (Stanley Fish's expression), discerning how material forms affect meaning, localizing social difference in practices more than in statistical distributions – these are the routes laid out for anyone who wishes to understand as a historian the 'silent production' that is 'the activity of reading'.[31]

2

Figures of the Author

D. F. McKenzie has stressed the fundamental kinship between bibliography (in its classic definition of a study of the physical aspects of the book) and all forms of structuralist criticism, noting, 'The congruence of bibliography and criticism lay precisely in their shared view of the self-sufficient nature of the work of art or text. . . . In neither case were precedent or subsequent processes thought to be essential to critical or bibliographical practice.'[1] For both the New Criticism and analytical bibliography, the production of meaning relied on the automatic and impersonal operation of a system of signs – either the system instituting the language of the text or the one organizing the form of the printed object. Consequently, both approaches refused to consider that the manner in which a work is read, received, and interpreted has any importance for establishing its meaning, and both proclaimed 'the death of the author' (as Barthes titled his famous essay) and stripped authorial intention of any special pertinence. In this perspective, dominant in the English-speaking world (Great Britain, the United States, Australia, New Zealand), the history of the book was thus a history with neither readers nor authors. What it saw as essential was the process of the fabrication of the book, a process apprehended from traces left in the object itself and explained by editorial decisions, printshop practices, and the customs of the print trade. Paradoxically (if one remembers that the first goal of a study of the material aspects of the book has traditionally been to establish and publish correct and authentic texts),[2] bibliographic tradition has contributed greatly to the effacement of the author that was characteristic of the hegemony of semiotics.

In France, where the history of the book was more immediately cultural and social, the perspective could have been (perhaps should have been) different, but the historians' primary interests bore it elsewhere.[3] Scholars were more interested in ascertaining wealth, alliances, and hierarchies in the milieu of those who manufactured and sold books: merchant-booksellers, printers, compositors and pressmen, type founders, engravers, bookbinders, and others. Historians attempted to reconstruct the circulation of books, inequalities in book ownership among the various groups in society, and the impact of the book on mentalities. This approach privileged a quantitative treatment of massive data sets, relying on such materials as lists of books contained in probate inventories, catalogues printed for public auction sales of libraries, or, when historians had the good luck to come across them in the archives, booksellers' account books. It focused, if not on reading practices, at least on the sociology of readers. The author was forgotten in French history of the book as in the Anglo-Saxon bibliographic tradition – somewhat paradoxically when we recall Lucien Febvre's and Henri-Jean Martin's original programme 'to examine the influence and the practical significance of the printed book during the first 300 years of its existence'.[4] In the tradition of the social history of print as it has developed in France, books have readers but they do not have authors – or, more precisely, authors do not enter into that history's domain of competence: they are wholly the province of literary history and its time-honoured genres – biography, the study of a school or a current, or the description of an intellectual milieu.

Whether the history of the book neglects the author or leaves him or her to others, it has been practised as if its techniques and discoveries were irrelevant to the history of those who produced texts, or as if that history had no importance for the comprehension of works. In recent years, however, we have seen the return of the author. Literary criticism has distanced itself from points of view exclusively focused on the internal operation of the system of signs that constitutes a text, and it has attempted to set works back within their history. This move has taken various forms. The 'aesthetic of reception' aimed at describing the dialogue between an individual work and its readers' 'horizon of expectations', defined as the set of conventions and references shared by the work's public or publics. This approach, far from taking the meaning of the text as stable, univocal, and universal, thus comprehended it as historically constructed and as produced in the dialogue that exists between the propositions contained in the work (which are in part controlled by the author's intentions) and the readers' responses.[5] The New Historicism is more interested in situating the literary work in relation to 'ordinary' texts (of a practical, juridical, political, or religious nature) that constitute the raw materials on which writing operates and that make its intelligibility possible.[6] With the sociology of cultural production, based on concepts forged by Pierre Bourdieu, analysis shifts to the laws of operation and the hierarchies proper to a given field (literary, artistic, academic, religious, political, and so forth), to the structural relationships situating the various positions defined within a field, to the individual or collective strategies that those positions command, and to the transfer into the works themselves (in terms of genre, form, theme, and style) of the social conditions of their production.[7] Finally, the bibliography defined as a 'sociology of texts' proposed by D. F. McKenzie focuses on the way in which the physical forms through which texts are transmitted to their readers (or their auditors) affect the process of the construction of meaning. Understanding the reasons and the effects of such physical devices (for the printed book) as format, page layout, the way in which the text is broken up, the conventions governing its typographical presentation, and so forth, necessarily refers back to the control that the authors but sometimes the publishers exercised over the forms charged with expressing intention, orienting reception, and constraining interpretation.[8]

In spite of striking differences, even divergences among them, a common characteristic of all these approaches is that they reconnect the text with its author; the work with the intentions or the positions of its producer. This is of course not a restoration of the superb and solitary romantic figure of the sovereign author whose primary or final intention contains *the* meaning of the work and whose biography commands its writing with transparent immediacy. As he returns in literary criticism or literary sociology the author is both dependent and constrained. He is dependent in that he is not the unique master of the meaning of his text, and his intentions, which provided the impulse to produce the text, are not necessarily imposed either on those who turn his text into a book (bookseller-publishers or print workers) or on those who appropriate it by reading it. He is constrained in that he undergoes the multiple determinations that organize the social space of literary production and that, in a more general sense, determine the categories and the experiences that are the very matrices of writing.

The multifaceted return of the author in critical problematics takes us back to the question that Michel Foucault posed in a famous essay that has become an obligatory reference: What is an author?[9] In this essay Foucault distinguished between the 'sociohistorical analysis of the author's persona' and the more fundamental problem of the construction of an 'author-function' as a prime means of classifying discourses. Foucault states that, far from being universal or relevant to all texts in all ages, the attribution of a proper name to a work is a way of discriminating between texts. It is valid only for certain classes of texts ('The author-function is characteristic of the mode of existence, circulation, and functioning of certain discourses within a society'); it supposes a state of law that recognizes the author's penal responsibility and the concept of literary property ('The author-function is linked to the juridical and institutional system that encompasses, determines, and articulates the universe of discourses'). The author-function stands at some distance from the empirical evidence according to which every text has a redactor; it is the result of 'specific and complex operations' that put the unity, the coherence, and the inscription into historical context of a work (or a set of works) into relation with the identity of a constructed subject. This operation relies on a dual process of selection. First, the texts assignable to the author-function must be separated from the many texts that an individual may produce ('How can one define a work amid the millions of traces left by someone after his death?'). Second, one must pick from among the innumerable events that constitute a biography and must retain the facts pertinent to a definition of the author's position.

Although it is not his prime objective, Foucault sketches a history of the emergence of (and variations on) the attribution of texts by identification with a proper name – the name of the author – endowed with a quite specific function. In the original version of 'Qu'est-ce qu'un auteur?' Foucault outlined three chronological stages. The first, and the only one that commentators remark on with any frequency, is the time when 'a system of ownership for texts came into being ... strict rules concerning author's rights, author–publisher relations, rights of reproduction, and related matters were enacted – at the end of the eighteenth and the beginning of the nineteenth century'. This strong connection between the individuality of the author and the inscription of the activity of writing and publishing within the regime of private property is not, however, the founding principle of the author-function. The function is older and rooted in other determinations:

> We should note that, historically, this type of ownership has always been subsequent to what one might call penal appropriation. Texts, books, and discourses really began to have authors (other than mythical, 'sacralized' and 'sacralizing' figures) to the extent that authors became subject to punishment, that is, to the extent that discourses could be transgressive.

Foucault proposes no date for that 'penal appropriation' linking the author-function to the exercise of power by an authority with the right to censor, judge, and punish rather than, as formerly, to the juridical conventions regulating relations between private individuals. A third remark none the less hints that, thus defined, the author-function predates the modern world.

To illustrate the point that 'the author-function does not affect all discourses in a universal and constant way', Foucault evokes the radical reversal that, according to him, 'occurred in the seventeenth century or eighteenth century', when rules for the attribution of texts belonging to 'scientific' and 'literary' discourse were exchanged. After that watershed moment, the authority of scientific statements was founded on 'their membership in a systematic ensemble' of pre-established truths rather than on reference to particular authors; 'literary discourse', on the other hand, 'came to be accepted only when endowed with the author-function'. Formerly the reverse had been true:

> There was a time when the texts that we today call 'literary' (narratives, stories, epics, tragedies, comedies) were accepted, put into circulation, and valorized without any question about the identity of their author; their anonymity caused no difficulties since their ancientness, whether real or imagined, was regarded as a sufficient guarantee of their status. On the other hand, those texts that we now would call scientific – those dealing with cosmology and the heavens, medicine and illnesses, natural sciences and geography – were accepted in the Middle Ages, and accepted as 'true,' only when marked with the name of their author.

It is not my intention to debate the validity of the change that Foucault notes in this passage but rather to note that he recognizes that, for certain classes of texts, reference to the author was functional as early as the Middle Ages. A hasty reading must not lead us to reduce Foucault's thought to oversimplified formulas: in no way does he

postulate an exclusive and determinant connection between literary property and the author-function; between
'the system of property that characterizes our society' and
a system for the attribution of texts founded on the category of the subject. By moving the figure of the author
back in time and by articulating it with mechanisms for
controlling the circulation of texts or for lending them
authority, Foucault's essay invites us to a retrospective
investigation that gives the history of the conditions of
the production, dissemination, and appropriation of texts
particular pertinence.

Such a history would lead – and in fact has led in
several recent studies – to a reconsideration of the context
in which the concept of literary property first appeared.[10]
The first major revision suggested that the affirmation of
literary ownership, far from arising from a particular
application of a modern individual property law, derived
directly from the book trade's defence of permissions to
print – authorizations that guaranteed exclusive rights to
a work to the bookseller who had obtained title to it. In
England and in France, it was really the monarchy's
attempts to limit the *privilèges*, which traditionally granted
perpetual rights, that led the bookseller-publishers to link
the irrevocability of their rights to recognition of the
author's ownership of his or her work. The strategy of the
London booksellers' opposition to the Statute of 1709,
which set a fourteen-year limit on copyrights (prolonged
for another fourteen years if the author was still alive), has
points of similarity with Diderot's strategy in the 1760s
when he defended Paris booksellers who were concerned
that perpetual renewals of their *privilèges* might be done
away with. The London booksellers attempted to safe-
guard the perpetuity of their copyrights by treating the
property rights of the author who ceded a manuscript to

them as a common law right. Diderot attempted to profit from the opportunity offered him to demonstrate authors' full literary property by presenting the *privilège* as a perpetual right of ownership rather than as a favour accorded by the sovereign. Diderot states: 'I repeat: the author is master of his work or no one in society is master of his wealth. The bookseller possesses it as it was possessed by the author.' Thus for Diderot the writer's ownership founded the legitimacy of the *privilège*; conversely, it was the imprescriptibility of the *privilège* that manifested the author's rights.[11] Thus what Mark Rose has to say about England might well be applied to France: 'It might be said that the London booksellers invented the modern proprietary author, constructing him as a weapon in their struggle with the booksellers of the provinces'[12] – those same provincial booksellers whose activities depended almost entirely on reprints made possible by the suppression of perpetual permissions accorded to the powerful booksellers of the two capitals.

When the governing powers recognized the authors' rights over their works, they did so in the ancient logic of the *privilège*. This was true in the case with the Statute of 1709, which attempted to break the monopoly of the London booksellers by giving authors the right to demand a copyright themselves. It was also the case in France with the decree of the king's council of 1777 that stated that the book trade *privilège* was a 'grace founded in justice' (not founded by 'a rightful proprietorship') and that the permissions that the author had obtained in his own name were perpetual and patrimonial: 'He will enjoy his privilege, for himself and his heirs, in perpetuity.' In neither land did authors have an absolute right to their property – in England because of the limited duration of the copyright, even when granted to the author; in France because if the author ceded a manuscript to a bookseller, the latter's *privilège* (the minimum duration of which was ten years) was valid only 'during the life of the authors, in the event that they survive the expiration of the privileges'. In neither system of law was literary ownership equated with the ownership of real property, which was inalienable and freely transmissible.

Thus literary ownership had to be justified, whether it was considered absolute by booksellers who used the concept in defence of perpetual privileges and copyrights or whether it was considered limited by the state, which recognized it in order to allow the constitution of a public domain in printing. The 1777 law states, for example, that 'all booksellers and printers may obtain, after the expiration of the *privilège* for a work and the death of its author, a permission to print an edition without the granting of this permission to one or several persons preventing anyone else from obtaining a similar permission'. In the debates and lawsuits involving book trade permissions in England, France and Germany, two systems for legitimizing the author's rights were used, either simultaneously or concurrently. The first, explicitly or implicitly founded on a reference to the theory of natural law as formulated by Locke, considered the author's ownership to be the fruit of individual labour. This theme appeared in 1725 in a memoir that the booksellers' and printers' guild in Paris, eager to defend *privilèges* even at that early date, commissioned from the jurist Louis d'Héricourt. The memoir states that the work produced by an author is 'the fruit of a labour that is personal to him, which he must have the liberty to dispose of at will'.[13] The same thought runs through the arguments of the London booksellers: 'Labour gives a man a natural right of property in that which he produces: literary

compositions are the effect of labour; authors have therefore a natural right of property in their works.'[14] In
France, the decree of the king's council of August 1777
implicitly linked the perpetuity of the permissions accorded to authors and the specificity of their 'labour':

> His Majesty has recognized that the book trade privilege
> is a grace founded in justice that has as its object, if it is
> accorded to the author, to reward his labour; if it is ob-
> tained by a bookseller, to assure him the reimbursement of
> his advance payments and compensation for his expenses,
> so that this difference in the reasons determining a priv-
> ilege will produce [a difference] in its duration.

Hence the 'more extended grace' that was accorded to
authors. Whether they were considered to reflect full proprietorship or compensation, the author's rights over his
work found basic justification in the assimilation of writing
to labour.

The need for a second system of legitimation arose out
of objections raised to the very notion of a private appropriation of ideas. In England the adversaries of perpetual
copyright held that literary works should be treated in the
same way as 'mechanical' inventions. Such critics argued
that both were produced by assembling elements available
to everyone and should therefore be subjected to similar
legislation, hence copyrights should be limited to fourteen
years just as patents for the exclusive exploitation of technological inventions were: 'A mechanic Invention, and a
literary Composition, exactly agree in Point of Similarity;
the one therefore is no more entitled to be the object of
Common Law Property than the other.'[15] In France, as
Carla Hesse has shown, men such as Condorcet or Sieyès
held unlimited literary property to be unjust because ideas

belonged to everyone, and held it contrary to the progress of Enlightenment because it instituted one person's monopoly over a body of knowledge that should be for the common good. Thus, they argued, literary property should not be absolute but rather the public interest dictated that it should be severely limited.[16]

To parry arguments of this sort the champions of authors' exclusive and perpetual rights shifted the basic criterion of those rights. They argued that although ideas could be held in common and shared widely, the same was not true of the form in which the irreducible singularity of style and sentiment was expressed. The legitimation of literary property was thus based on a new aesthetic perception designating the work as an original creation recognizable by the specificity of its expression. This concept combining a unique form, the author's genius, and the inalienability of the author's ownership was argued during the conflicts engendered in England by the Statute of 1709, in particular by William Blackstone in *Tonson* v. *Collins* in 1760. It found its most radical formulations in open polemics in Germany between 1773 and 1794 in which (as was also true in France and England) discussion of book trade privileges was linked to a debate about the very nature of literary creation. The controversy, to which such writers as Zacharias Becker, Kant, Fichte, and Herder contributed, resulted in a new definition of the work, now no longer characterized by the ideas that it embodied (since ideas cannot be the object of individual appropriation) but by its *form* – that is, by the particular way in which an author produces, assembles, expresses, and presents concepts.[17] The text, which results from an organic process comparable to Nature's creations and is invested with an aesthetic of originality, transcends the circumstantial materiality of the book – a transcendence

that distinguishes it from a technological invention[18] –
and it acquires an identity immediately referable to the
subjectivity of its author rather than to divine presence,
tradition, or genre. This theory of the work prefigures the
main traits of the author-function as Foucault presents it,
where the author is 'the principle of a certain unity of
writing' different from all others and 'a particular source of
expression' manifested in all the creations attributed to that
author.

Thus in the latter half of the eighteenth century a somewhat paradoxical connection was made between a desired
professionalization of literary activity (which should provide remuneration in order for writers to live from their
writings) and the authors' representation of themselves in
an ideology of literature founded on the radical autonomy
of the work of art and the disinterestedness of the creative
act.[19] On the one hand, the poetic or philosophic work
became a negotiable commodity endowed with a *valeur
commerçante*, as Diderot put it, hence could be the object of
a contract and evaluated in monetary terms. On the other
hand, the work was held to result from a free and inspired
activity motivated by its internal necessities alone. When
authors shifted from the patronage system (where retribu-
tion for their writing usually preceded the act of writing in
the form of a sinecure or followed it in the form of
gratifications) to operate in the market, where immediate
and monetary profit was expected from the sale of a
manuscript to a bookseller (or, for a dramatist, from a
percentage of the proceeds of performances of his plays),
this shift was accompanied by an apparently contradictory
change in the ideology of writing, henceforth defined by
the urgency and absolute freedom of creative power.[20]

The connection established between inspiration and
merchandise doubly reversed the traditional view of

literary activity. The notion that 'Glory is the Reward of
Science, and those who deserve it, scorn all meaner
Views'[21] prompted the objection that it was simple justice
for the labour of writing to involve pecuniary profit. Formerly, dependency was the norm for authors with neither
a public office nor independent means; now that dependency stood in stark contrast to the consubstantial independence of all creative invention.[22] A radical reversal
different from the one discussed by Foucault thus seems to
have occurred during the latter half of the eighteenth
century. Before, the author's subjection to obligations created by client relations and patronage ties was accompanied
by a radical incommensurability between literary works and
economic transactions. After the mid-century the situation
was reversed when a possible and necessary monetary appreciation of literary compositions, remunerated as labour
and subject to the laws of the market, was founded on an
ideology of creative and disinterested genius that guaranteed the originality of the work.

It is tempting to draw a close connection between the
modern definition of the author and the resources (or the
demands) inherent in the publication of printed texts. In
his study of Samuel Johnson, whose life Boswell's biography made 'the model of the poetic role in the age of
print', Alvin Kernan stresses the relationship between the
constitution of a market for works – a market that only
printing could make possible – and the affirmation of the
author. In the 'new print-based, author-centered literary
system' in late eighteenth-century England the author – at
least the successful author – could enjoy a financial
independence that freed him from the obligations of
patronage and enabled him to acknowledge his published
works. This new model broke with the classic figure of
the gentleman writer or the gentleman amateur formerly

accepted even by writers who were by no means of aristocratic birth. In the traditional definition, the author lived not by the pen but from investments and landholdings or public office; he scorned print and expressed an aristocratic 'antipathy to a medium that perverted the primary courtly literary values of privacy and rarity'; he preferred the chosen public of his peers, manuscript circulation for his works, and concealment of his name in an anonymous work. When recourse to printing became unavoidable the effacement of the author that was typical of the 'courtly tradition of anonymity' took several forms. The author might choose to leave his name off the title page (as with Swift). He might use the fictional device of a manuscript found by chance: Thomas Gray wrote, speaking of his *Elegy in a Country Churchyard*, 'If [the printer] would add a Line or two to say it came into his Hands by Accident, I should like it better.' Or he might create an apocryphal author: Thomas Rowley, a monk from Bristol, was the declared author of poems actually written by Thomas Chatterton, and James MacPherson invented a Celtic bard, Ossian, presenting himself as merely the translator of the works he had in fact written. These values and practices characteristic of the 'literary ancien régime' had been undermined, however, by 'a new world of letters based on the realities of print technology and its market economics'. The new economics of writing supposed the full visibility of the author, the original creator of a work from which he could legitimately expect to profit.[23]

Definitions in French-language dictionaries of the latter seventeenth century seem to confirm the association between the author and print publication. In 1690 Furetière's *Dictionnaire universel* gave seven meanings for the word *auteur*, and the one concerning *la littérature* came only in sixth place, after definitions in the realms of philosophy and religion ('one who has created or produced something. Said par excellence of the first Cause which is God'), technical ('said in particular of those who are the first Inventors of something'), practical ('said also of those who are the cause of something'), political ('said also of Leaders of a party, an opinion, a conspiracy, or a rumour going about'), and genealogical ('the *author* of the race of a house, of a family'). It precedes the juridical definition: 'In terms of the Palace [of Justice], one calls *Authors* Those who have acquired the right to possess some inheritance by sale, exchange, donation, or other contract.' The word is thus not immediately invested with a literary meaning, its first uses situating it in the register of natural creation, material invention, and a chain of connected actions. When it arrives at the literary meaning, the *Dictionnaire universel* specifies, '*Author*, in literature, is said of all those who have brought some book into the light. Now one says it only of those who have had a book or books printed.' The dictionary adds as an example of the use of the term, 'That man finally has risen to be an *Author*; has been printed.' The term 'author' presupposed printed circulation of works and, in return, recourse to the press distinguished the 'author' from the 'writer', whom Furetière defines without reference to printing: '*Escrivain*, is said also of those who have composed Books, Works.'

Ten years before Furetière, the *Dictionnaire Français* of Richelet had already established a necessary connection between the author and printing in its second definition of the word (after the prime meaning of 'the first who has invented something, who has said something, who is cause of something that has been done'). The entry reads: 'He who has composed some printed book', and it is followed by illustrative examples: 'Ablancour, Pascal, Voiture, and Vaugelas are excellent French Authors. Queen Marguerite, the daughter of Henry III, was an author.'[24] In his series of examples Furetière also takes care to mention the presence of women among authors: 'One says also of a woman that she has risen [*s'est érigée*] as an Author when she has made some book or theatrical work.'[25] For these two dictionaries of the late seventeenth century, the term 'author' is not to be applied to anyone who writes a work; the term distinguishes among all 'writers' only those who have cared to have their compositions published. Writing was not enough if one wanted to *s'ériger en auteur*; one's work also had to circulate in public by means of print.

We find this relationship expressed in the late seventeenth century, but was it even older? One answer to the question comes from the first two catalogues of French-language authors published in France, the *Premier Volume de la Bibliothèque du Sieur de La Croix du Maine* (1584) and *La Bibliothèque d'Antoine du Verdier, seigneur de Vauprivas* (1585).[26] The long subtitle of the *Bibliothèque* of La Croix du Maine is clearly organized on the basis of the category of the author: 'Which is a general catalogue of all sorts of authors who have written in French for five hundred years and more until this day: with a Discourse on the lives of the most illustrious and renowned among the three thousand who are included in this work, together with a relation of their compositions both printed and other.' The author-function already has its basic characteristics here. For one thing, La Croix du Maine makes authorship the first criterion of classification of works that have no other distribution than names in alphabetical order – or rather, in the medieval manner, of their author's first names, since the *Bibliothèque* runs from 'Abel

Foulon' to 'Yves Le Fortier', with a table of contents to aid retrieval of the authors on the basis of their last names. Further, in proposing 'lives' of the authors (which, incidentally, do not figure in volume one of the *Bibliothèque*, the only volume to have been published), La Croix du Maine sets up the writer's biography as the fundamental reference for writing. This primacy given to the author, defined as a real individual whose life can be related, is confirmed by Antoine Du Verdier, whose *Bibliothèque* 'containing the catalogue of all those who have written or translated in French and other Dialects of this Realm' excludes fictive authors: 'I have not wanted to put in it the Almanacs of various sorts that have been made annually under supposed names. Given even that correctors in printing establishments made them, for the most part, in the name of persons who never were.'

The two *Bibliothèques* of La Croix du Maine and Du Verdier attest that the deployment of the author-function was not necessarily connected either with print publication or with the independence of the writer. Both of them, unlike Richelet and Furetière in their definitions of a century later, consider that the manuscript makes the author just as much as the printed book. In fact, the two compilations announce in their titles that they will mention, for all authors, 'their compositions both printed and other' (La Croix du Maine) or 'all of their works printed and not printed' (Du Verdier). La Croix du Maine, justifying the usefulness of his catalogue as a means for preventing usurpers from publishing under their own name works remaining in manuscript at their true author's death, specifies, 'inasmuch as I have spoken of both printed works and those that are not yet in the light [*en lumière*]'. At the end of the sixteenth century in France, if the category of the author constituted the basic principle for classifying discourse, it did not obligatorily presuppose their *mise en lumière*, that is, their existence in print.

The author-function had no trouble harmonizing with the dependency instituted by patronage. In a dedication addressed to the king, La Croix du Maine mentions his two reasons for publishing the *Premier Volume* of his *Bibliothèque*. The first was to show the superiority of the Kingdom of France with its three thousand authors who had written in the vernacular, whereas the authors who had written or translated into Italian numbered no more than three hundred.[27] The second was 'to have the friendship of so many learned men who are living today *of whom the greater part are employed in the service of your Majesty*' (emphasis mine). The detail attests that the construction of the author-function was quite conceivable within the modalities that characterized the 'literary ancien régime'. Far from being contradictory, the patronage connection and the affirmation of the author together define the regime of assignation of texts. La Croix du Maine clearly expressed this when in 1579 he wrote of his *Grande Bibliothèque Françoise*, volume five of which, published five years later, was a simple *Epitomé*. *La Grande Bibliothèque Françoise*, which was never printed, was not only to contain 'the catalogue of the works or writings of every author' but also indicated for all works 'by whom they were printed, in what format or size, in what years, how many sheets they contain, *and especially the names of the men or women to whom they were dedicated, without omitting all their entire qualities*' (emphasis mine). As on a title page, every work was thus referred to the names of three persons, the author, the dedicatee, and the bookseller or printer-publisher, reinforced by his mark.[28]

The title page of the editio princeps of *Don Quixote* in 1605 illustrates this well.[29] At the top is the title in capital letters: EL INGENIOSO / HIDALGO DON QUI/ XOTE DE LA MANCHA. Underneath this, in italics, comes the essential assignment of the text, '*Compuesto por Miguel de Cervantes / Saavedra*'. (This information is repeated in the preliminary materials along with the *tasa* indicating the price at which the book can be sold – 'doscientos y noventa maravedís y medio' – and the *licencia*, which accords the author a printing privilege for ten years.) Under the author's name, in roman letters, is the mention of the dedicatee with his titles in full: 'DIRIGIDO AL DUQUE DE BEIAR, / Marques de Gibraleon, Conde de Benalcaçar, y Baña-/res, Vizconde de la Puebla de Alcozer, Señor de / las villas de Capilla, Curiel, y / Burguillos.' The upper third of the title page is thus given over to the fundamental relationship that dominated literary activity until the mid eighteenth century: the connecting of an author (already constituted as such) to a protector from whom he expected support and gratifications. The printer's mark, framed by the two elements of the date, 'Año' and '1605', occupies the greater part of the remaining space. At the bottom there are three lines of text: 'CON PRIVILEGIO, / *EN MADRID*, Por Juan de la Cuesta. / Vendese en casa de Francisco de Robles, librero del Rey nño señor.' These provide the proper indications to satisfy the requirements of the book trade: mention of the privilege, the mark of royal authority, the place of publication and the name of the printer and, at the very bottom under a solid horizontal line, the address at which an eventual buyer could buy the work.

The very construction of the visual space of the title page expresses several things that are less contradictory and earlier in date than is sometimes thought. The first is an affirmation of the author's literary paternity, recognized by the king who accords Cervantes the *licencia y facultad* to print or have printed a work 'that cost him great labour and is most useful and profitable'. The same paternity is displayed with irony by Cervantes in his prologue: 'Pero yo, que, aunque parezco padre, soy padrastro de don Quijote, no quiero irme con la corriente de uso, ni suplicarte casi con las lágrimas en los ojos, como otros hacen, lector carísimo, que perdones o disimules las faltas que en este mi hijo vieres' (But I, though in appearance Don Quixote's father, am really his step-father, and so will not drift with the current of custom, nor implore you, almost with tears in my eyes, as others do, dearest reader, to pardon or ignore the faults you see in this child of mine).[30] The play on the words *padre* and *padrastro* is a way to prefigure the fiction introduced in chapter 9, the first chapter in the 'Segunda Parte' of the 1605 *Quixote*, in which the narrative offered the reader is in fact a translation into Castilian done 'en poco más de mes y medio' (in little more than six weeks) by a Morisco from Toledo of a manuscript in Arabic, the *Historia de don Quijote de la Mancha, escrita por Cide Hamete Benengeli, historiador arábigo*.[31] Neither the theme of the text encountered by chance (in this case, found amid the 'cartapacios y papeles viejos' – 'parchments and old papers' – sold by a lad to a silk merchant) nor that of the pre-existent work of which the published book simply offers a copy or a translation is used here to disguise the real author. The 'authors' of the novel multiply: there is the 'I' of the prologue who announces that the work is his; then there is the author of the eight first chapters who upsets the 'I-reader' inscribed in the text when he suddenly interrupts his narration ('This caused me great annoyance');

there is also the author of the Arabic manuscript; finally, there is the Morisco author of the translation that is the text read by the 'I-reader' and by the reader of the novel. What this break-up of the author does, however, is to manifest the figure of the author in its primordial function of guaranteeing the unity and the coherence of the discourse.

The title page of *Don Quixote* is equally unambiguous in its presentations of patronage (with the dedication to the duke of Bejar) and the market (with the mention of the printer, Juan de la Cuesta, to whom Cervantes had ceded the *licencia y facultad* to print his book accorded to the author by a royal cedula dated 26 September 1604). The author's desire to participate in market logic and to have control over the sale of his works to a bookseller or a printer who will publish them is totally compatible with an acceptance of or a search for patronage. One example of this (among others) in Elizabethan England is the case of Ben Jonson. Jonson affirmed (and exercised) the author's right to sell his works directly to a publisher, contradicting a long-standing custom that granted theatrical companies an exclusive right to have copied or printed the manuscripts of the plays they put on. Thus he seized control of his own texts in view of publication (as for the edition of the *Workes of Benjamin Jonson* published by William Stansby in 1616). Ben Jonson also counts among the first English authors who dedicated their published plays to aristocratic patrons: *The Masque of Queenes* was dedicated to Prince Henry in 1609, *Catiline* to the Count of Pembroke in 1611, and *The Alchemist* to Mary Wroth in 1612. Patronage and the market were thus not mutually exclusive, and all authors of the sixteenth and seventeenth centuries faced the same need as Ben Jonson: to adapt 'the modern technology of dissemination to an archaic patronage economy'.[32]

Contracts between authors and booksellers confirm this dovetailing of the rules of commerce and the need for protection. In the thirty or so contracts that Annie Parent-Charron has found for Paris in the years 1535–60 the commonest case has the bookseller taking responsibility for all the printing costs and for obtaining the *privilège* and the author receiving as remuneration free copies of the book ranging in number from twenty-five copies for the translation of Livy's *Décades* by Jean de Amelin published by Guillaume Cavellat (in a contract dated 6 August 1658) to one hundred copies for the *Epithome de la vraye astrologie et de la réprovée* of David Finarensis printed by Etienne Groulleau (contract dated 22 August 1547). A monetary remuneration added to the free copies from the bookseller appears only in two situations, when the author obtained the *privilège* and paid the chancery fees, and when the contract covers a translation, especially in the years 1550–60 for the Castilian chivalric romances that were all the rage. Even in that case, the consignment of copies that could be offered to the king or to grandees (actual or potential patrons) remained the most important element. Proof of this is a clause in the contract dated 19 November 1540 between Nicolas de Herberay and the Paris booksellers Jean Longis and Vicent Sertenas for Herberay's translation of the second, third, and fourth parts of *Amadis de Gaule*. For his labours and for the *privilège* that Herberay himself had obtained, he received not only 80 écus d'or soleil and twelve copies of each book *en blanc en volume de feuille* (in unbound sheets) but also an exclusive right to distribute the book for a limited time: the contract states that booksellers 'can distribute or sell any of the said three volumes only after they have first been presented by the said Herberay to the King our Lord, on pain of all expenses and damages and interests, which he promises to present six weeks after the said fourth volume will have been delivered to him printed in sheets as stated' – a delay that would give the author time to have the presentation copies properly bound.[33]

The traditional system of patronage, far from being dismantled by the diffusion of the printed book, adapted to the new technique for the reproduction of texts and to the market logic that it set up. This is true for the Renaissance, and it was probably still partially true in the eighteenth century, at the time of the first 'professionalization' of authors who were eager and at times capable of living (not necessarily well) by their pens. As Robert Darnton has shown in his analysis of the list of writers kept under surveillance by Inspector of Police d'Hémery between 1748 and 1753 and the survey of *gens de lettres* published in *La France littéraire* in 1784, the two ancient models for the author's condition remained dominant: the writer either enjoyed an economic independence assured by birth or profession or lived on gratifications and sinecures procured from patronage.[34] The new phenomenon of a social status founded solely on the remuneration of writing emerged only with difficulty within the mental framework of the ancien régime, a situation expressed by Voltaire in his diatribes against 'the miserable species that writes for a living'. Freedom (of ideas or of commerce) seemed in no way contradictory to the protection of authority, beginning with the protection of the king, dispenser of positions and favours.

Since the emergence of the author-function is less directly connected to the definition of the concept of literary property than might be thought, must it then be attached to 'penal appropriation' of discourses? To the writer's judicial responsibility? Or, as Foucault writes, to 'the danger of writing' when writing had become subject to criminal prosecution?[35] Answering this question and exploring the complex and multiple relations between state and church censorship and the construction of the figure of the author is far beyond the scope of the present study. Let me cite one example, though. In France after 1544 catalogues of the books that had been censored by the Faculty of Theology of Paris began to be published. In all editions of this catalogue (1544, 1545, 1547, 1551, 1556) titles are arranged in the same manner, 'secundum ordinem alphabeticum juxta authorum cognomina'. The Sorbonne's Index used the category of the author as its fundamental principle for designating books in its lists of Latin works and French works. The 1544 catalogue begins with the rubrics 'Ex libris Andreae Althameri', 'Ex libris Martini Buceri', and so forth, maintaining its reference to the author even for anonymous books, which are enumerated under the titles 'Catalogus librorum quorum incerti sunt authores' (for Latin titles) and 'Catalogus librorum gallicorum ab incertis authoribus' (for French works).[36] In parallel fashion, the author's responsibility was introduced into royal legislation for controlling the printing, distribution, and sale of books. The edict of Chateaubriant of 27 June 1551, which marked the apogee of the collaboration between the king, the Parlement, and the Sorbonne regarding censorship, states in its article 8:

> It is forbidden to all printers to perform the exercise and status of impression except in good cities and orderly establishments accustomed to do this, not in secret places. And it must be under a master printer whose name,

domicile, and mark are put in the books thus printed by them [with] the time of the said impression and *the name of the author* [emphasis mine]. The which master printer will answer to faults and errors that either by him or under his name and by his order will have been made and committed.

The author-function was thus constituted as an essential weapon in the battle against the diffusion of texts suspected of heterodoxy.

In the repression of suspect books, however, the responsibility of the author of a censured book does not seem to have been considered any greater than that of the printer who published it, the bookseller or the pedlar who sold it, or the reader who possessed it. All could be led to the stake if they were convicted of having proffered or diffused heretical opinions. What is more, the acts of conviction often mix accusations concerning the printing and sale of censured books and accusations concerning the opinions – published or unpublished – of the perpetrator. This is what happened to Antoine Augereau, a type engraver who had become a printer, who was strangled and his body burned in the Place Maubert on 24 December 1534. The details of his sentence are not known but the chroniclers of the time explain the event by insisting on two points. First, they stress Augereau's printing activities (he was supposedly sentenced for having been an 'ally of bill-posters [of *placards* against the mass posted up during the night of 17–18 October 1534] and for having printed false books' as well as for having 'printed and sold books of Luther's'). Second, they insist on his heterodox opinions. One chronicle brands Augereau as 'Lutheran', and the judgement of the Parlement refusing him the privilege of being tried before an ecclesiastical court (he was a cleric) specifies that he was 'charged with having said and proffered several erroneous, blasphemous, and scandalous propositions [the original has *prépositions*] against holy doctrine and the Catholic faith'.[37] Thus it was as an 'author' of heretical opinions as much as it was for his activities as a printer that Antoine Augereau was burned at the stake. Similarly, the accusations levelled against Etienne Dolet, a humanist who had become a printer, by the Sorbonne in 1543 mention not only the books that Dolet had printed or that merely were found in his house but also those that he had written or for which he had written a preface.[38] After the respite granted him by his abjuration on 13 November 1543, it was on the same charges (for having printed and sold prohibited books, having written unorthodox prefaces to several books) that Dolet was strangled and his body burned on 3 August on the Place Maubert, along with the censured books.[39]

In its connection with church or state censorship as in its association with literary property, the author-function is fully inscribed within the culture of print. In both cases it appears to derive from fundamental transformations brought by printing: it was printing that extended, hence that made more dangerous, the circulation of texts that defied authority, and printing created a market that presupposed the establishment of rules and conventions among all who profited from it, economically or symbolically, the writer, the bookseller-publisher, and the printer. But was this really the case? Perhaps not, if we acknowledge that the essential traits in the book that manifest the assignation of the text to a particular individual designated as its author do not make their first appearance with printed works but were already typical of the manuscript book at the end of its unchallenged reign.

The most spectacular of those traits is the physical representation of the author in his book. The portrait of the author, which makes the assignation of the text to a single 'I' immediately visible, is frequent in printed books of the sixteenth century.[40] Whether or not the image endows the author (or the translator) with real or symbolic attributes of his (or her) art, whether presented in heroic classical style or 'from life', in natural appearance, the function of the author's portrait is to reinforce the notion that the writing is the expression of an individuality that gives authenticity to the work. However, representations of the author – and often of the author shown in the act of writing – appear in miniatures decorating manuscripts in the vernacular of the late fourteenth and the fifteenth centuries. This is true of works of Christine de Pisan, Jean Froissart, and René d'Anjou, and of Petrarch and Boccaccio. Portraits of the sort were novelties in two ways. First, at a time when the French words *escrire* and *escripvain* took on their modern meanings to indicate not only the copying but also the composition of texts, such portraits show an autograph writing that no longer presupposes dictation to a secretary. Second, they transfer to contemporary authors who wrote in the vulgar tongue the theme, frequent since the early fourteenth century in Latin texts, of writing as individual invention and original creation. The new image broke with time-honoured conventions in representations of the process of writing, both the convention that equated writing with listening to a dictated text and copying it (for example in the traditional iconography of the Evangelists and the Fathers of the church figured as scribes of the Divine Word) and the convention that thought of writing as a simple continuation of an existing work (as in the

EL INGENIOSO
HIDALGO DON QVI-
Y. 1100. XOTE DE LA MANCHA,
2.
Compueſto por Miguel de Ceruantes
Saauedra.

DIRIGIDO AL DVQVE DE BEIAR,
Marques de Gibraleon, Conde de Benalcaçar, y Baña-
res, Vizconde de la Puebla de Alcozer, Señor de
las villas de Capilla, Curiel, y
Burguillos.

Año,   1605.

CON PRIVILEGIO,
EN MADRID, Por Iuan de la Cueſta.

Vendeſe en caſa de Franciſco de Robles, librero del Rey nro ſeñor.

Miguel de Cervantes, *El Ingenioso Hidalgo Don Quixote de la Mancha*, Madrid, Juan de la Cuesta, 1605, title page. (Source: Bibliothèque nationale, Imprimés.)

On the title page of the first edition of *Don Quixote* four proper names indicate who wrote the work, who received it in dedication, who published it, and who sold it.

Christophe de Savigny, *Tableaux accomplis de tous les arts libéraux*, Paris, Jean and François Gourmont, 1587, engraving. (Source: Roger-Viollet.)

The work offered in homage was expected to elicit gratifications and positions for its author from the already conquered or courted protector.

Opposite: Pierre de Ronsard, *Les Oeuvres*, Paris, Gabriel Buon, 1567, vol. 1, engraving, fol. Aaa 8v. (Source: Roger-Viollet.)

Heroicized in the ancient style and crowned with laurel, the living portrait of the Poet presented in both his verse and his image.

Tel fut Ronſard, autheur de ceſt ouurage,
Tel fut ſon œil, ſa bouche & ſon viſage,
Portrait au vif de deux crayons diuers:
Jcy le Corps, & l'Eſprit en ſes vers.

Boccaccio, *Livre des cent nouvelles*, Paris, Antoine Vérard, 1485, prologue. (Source: Bibliothèque nationale, Imprimés.)

The author, identified by name (Bocace), himself writing, composing the text given to his reader to read.

Opposite: Etienne-Louis Boullée, *Deuxième projet pour la Bibliothèque du Roi*, Paris, 1785. (Source: Bibliothèque nationale, Estampes.)

Midway between utopian construction and architectural plan, Boullée imagines the King's Library as a gigantic basilica containing the entire memory of the world.

ADVIS
POVR DRESSER
VNE
BIBLIOTHEQVE.

Prefenté à Monfeigneur le
Prefident de MESME.

Par G. NAVDE' P.

Omnia quæ magna funt atque admirabilia,
tempus aliquod quo primùm efficerentur
habuerunt.   *Quintil. lib.* 12.

A PARIS,

Chez FRANÇOIS TARGA, au premier
pillier de la grand'Salle du Palais,
deuant les Confultations.

M. DC. XXVII.

Auec Priuilege du Roy.

Gabriel Naudé, *Advis pour dresser une bibliothèque*, Paris, Rolet le Duc, 1627, title page. (Source: Bibliothèque nationale, Imprimés.)

In its small format, the second edition (1644) of the most famous guide for creating a 'universal' library for public use.

PREMIER VOLVME DE

LA BIBLIOTHEQVE
DV SIEVR DE LA CROIX·DV MAINE.

Qui est vn catalogue general de toutes sortes d'Autheurs, qui ont escrit en
François depuis cinq cents ans & plus, iusques à ce iourd'huy : auec
vn Discours des vies des plus illustres & renommez entre les
trois mille qui sont compris en cet œuure, ensemble
vn recit de leurs compositions, tant impri-
mees qu'autrement.

DEDIÉ ET PRESENTÉ AV ROY.

Sur la fin de ce liure se voyent les desseins & proiects dudit sieur de la CROIX, lesquels il presenta
au Roy l'an 1583 pour dresser vne Bibliotheque parfaite & accomplie en toutes sortes.

Dauantage se voit le Discours de ses œuures & compositions, imprimé derechef
sur la copie qu'il fist mettre en lumiere l'an 1579.

A PARIS,

Chez Abel l'ANGELIER, Libraire Iuré tenant sa boutique au premier
pillier de la grand Salle du Palais.

M. D. LXXXIIII.

AVEC PRIVILEGE DV ROY.

Premier volume de la Bibliothèque du Sieur La Croix du Maine, Paris, Abel
l'Angelier, 1584, title page. (Source: Bibliothèque nationale,
Imprimés.)

Dedicated to Henry III, the only work ever published by La Croix du
Maine, bringing together his catalogue of French authors, his project
for the King's Library, and a list of the works that he states he wrote.

Raphael, *The School of Athens*, Vatican. (Source: Roger-Viollet.)

The full vigour of ancient knowledge set forth, dictated, and copied on the walls of the Stanza della Segnatura in the Vatican Palace.

case of the scholastic practice of the gloss and the commentary).[41]

That first and manifest form of the presence of the author in the book was accompanied by another less visible to the reader, which is the control exercised by the writer over the form of publication of the text. The edition of Congreve's *Works* published by Jacob Tonson in London in 1710 is emblematic of the author's intervention in the process of publishing his works. As we have seen in chapter 1, on the occasion of this octavo edition of his plays, which until then had been printed separately in a quarto format, Congreve gave new form to his texts, dividing them into scenes where they had been lacking and providing more stage directions with his dialogue. These innovations were reflected in the way in which the plays were printed by means of numbers for scenes, print ornaments placed between one scene and the next, a mention of the characters present given at the beginning of each scene, indications in the margin of who was speaking, and the notation of exits and entrances. These formal mechanisms, which were borrowed from French published theatrical works, gave a new status to the works, and that fact in turn led Congreve to prune his text of a few details that he considered contrary to the dignity of this new presentation.[42]

Contracts between printers and authors are another proof of the control that authors expected to exercise over the publication of their works. If sixteenth-century Paris can serve as an example, an author, as one might expect, had every reason to be demanding when he had a work printed and sold it himself, either directly or through a bookseller. Thus on 11 May 1559 Charles Périer, a merchant-bookseller and printer, promised a representative of the bishop of Laon, Jean Doc, to print and have printed, well and duly, as should be done, six volumes of the *Homélies des dimanches et festes de l'année* in the same letters and similar characters that the said Périer used formerly for the said Reverend gentleman [an allusion to other books printed by Périer for Jean Doc], and to do so in quarto volumes, and to adjust the annotations in it as they will be delivered to him.

Concern for the form of the book can also be seen when an author gave over his manuscript to a bookseller in exchange for free copies of the work and, at times, monetary remuneration. On 22 August 1547, when he contracted to print the *Epithome* of David Finarensis, Etienne Groulleau declared that he would respect 'the state in which he [Finarensis] wishes it to be printed, in the French language and with the type used in a piece of printed paper that he left in the hands of the said Finarensis, signed by the subscribed notaries, ne varietur'; on 29 November 1556 Ambroise de La Porte promised to print 'well and duly' a work of André Thevet entitled *Les singularitez de la France antarctique* and to 'have engraved figures in such terms as shall be agreed to between the said Thevet, de La Porte, and master Bernard de Poiseulne [the engraver]'; finally, on 3 April 1559 Frédéric Morel received several works composed or translated by Louis Le Roy, 'all to be printed correctly in handsome characters and [on] good paper, in large roman or italic letters'.[43] These agreements, which mention the typeface, the paper, the plates, and at times the format, attest clearly the authors' intention to establish their control over the way their texts were to circulate.

This intention was not born with print. In order to prevent his works from being corrupted by a division of labour between author and copyist so strict that he 'would no longer be able to recognize the texts he composed', Petrarch proposed another formula that would guarantee the author's domination of the production and transmission of the text. The 'author's book', produced from an autograph copy (not a scribe's copy), designed for limited circulation, and protected from the faulty copying of professional copyists, would manifest the author's intentions as the work had been composed with less risk of betraying those intentions or vitiating them. Controlled and stabilized in this manner, the text was to institute a direct and authentic relation between the author and the reader because, as Armando Petrucci tells us, 'perfect textuality, a direct emanation from the author validated by his autograph writing, was (and forever remained) a guarantee of absolute readability for the reader.'[44] Even though Petrarch's programme and his practice (he copied several of his own works in his own hand) remained out of the mainstream of the economy of production of the manuscript of his time, they none the less reflect an early emergence, in the fourteenth century, of one of the major expressions of the author-function, the possibility of deciphering in the forms of a book the intention that lay behind the creation of the text.

The more immediate and more material manifestation of the assignation of discourses to an author lies in the unity between a work and an object, between a textual unit and a codicological unit. This was long not true of works in the vulgar tongue. The dominant form of the manuscript book was, in fact, that of the notarial register or, in Italy, the *libro-zibaldone*. Such unadorned, small or medium-sized books, written in a cursive hand, were copied by their own readers, who put in them, in no apparent order, texts of quite different sorts in prose and in verse, devotional and technical, documentary and poetic. These compilations, produced by lay people unfamiliar with the traditional institutions of manuscript production and for whom the act of copying was a necessary preliminary to reading, characteristically show no sign of the author-function. The unity of such a book comes from the fact that its producer is also its addressee.[45] Even beyond this new public made up by readers who are not professionals of written culture (officials, notaries, secretaries), the form of the compilation, which was shared by a number of genres (*exempla*, *sententiae*, proverbs, fables, tales, lyric poetry, and so forth) helped to minimize assigning works to an individual. Thus among the three types of collections of lyric poetry of the fourteenth and fifteenth centuries discerned by Jacqueline Cerquiglini, only one (the one in which a poet gathers together his or her works) is fully qualifiable as displaying the author-function. The two other types (a collection of several poets' works in the form of an album and a collection in the form of an anthology) either present the texts anonymously or, when the authors' names are rubricated, construct the book's unity on the basis of the principle of a literary game played within a circle of friends or at a princely court that is a far cry from an individualized work.[46]

None the less, even before the age of the printed book (which incidentally prolonged the tradition of composite collections in a number of genres), the connection between a codicological unit and a textual unit ascribed to an author in his full singularity became true of certain works in the vulgar tongue. This was the case, for example, with Petrarch. A precise study shows how one of his major vernacular works, *I trionfi*, was transmitted in the manuscript tradition during the fourteenth and fifteenth centuries.[47] The first thing we note is that the manuscripts containing only texts by Petrarch (either only *I trionfi* or *I trionfi* along with the *Rerum Vulgarium Fragmenta* and/or other works) account for 62 per cent of the 424 manuscripts surveyed, whereas those in which Petrarch's text figures with the works of other authors represent 37 per cent of total books surveyed. Thus it is clear that during the last centuries of the hand-copied book, although a strong relationship existed between the book as an object and the author as a guarantee of the book's coherence, there were still signs, even with an author such as Petrarch, of the practice of the collection of works of mixed authorship. The second thing to note is that the author's singularity won out over the singularity of the work. In fact, the manuscripts that include only *I trionfi* represent 25 per cent of this total corpus, as against 37 per cent for those that combine two or several works by Petrarch (including his letters). The modern notion of 'book', which spontaneously associates an object and a work, although not unknown in the Middle Ages, separated off only slowly from the collection of several texts by a given author. A final remark: between the fourteenth and the fifteenth centuries the author-function clearly progresses in the identity of the book. Whereas in the 79 manuscripts in this corpus that come from the first half of the fourteenth century there is a nearly even balance between manuscripts containing only works by Petrarch and others mixing Petrarch's works with those of other authors (53 per cent and 46 per cent), the gap increases later in favour of manuscripts by Petrarch alone (63 per cent against 37 per cent) in the 248 manuscripts of the latter half of the fourteenth century, and 74 per cent against 26 per cent in the 78 manuscripts dating from the fifteenth century.

Foucault was right to recognize a presence of the author in the Middle Ages, when texts circulated in manuscript, but his hypothesis that authorship as a function for the classification of discourses was attached to medieval 'scientific' texts while 'literary' works fell under the rule of anonymity seems somewhat more fragile. In reality, a basic distinction must be made between the ancient texts – whatever their genre – that founded their authority on the work's attribution to a name (not only Pliny or Hippocrates, whom Foucault mentions, but also Aristotle and Cicero, St Jerome and St Augustine, Albert the Great and Vincent of Beauvais) and works in the vulgar tongue for which the author-function was constituted around a few great 'literary' figures – in Italy, Dante, Petrarch, and Boccaccio. In this sense, the trajectory of the author can be thought of as a gradual change in the way texts in the vernacular were regarded, attributing to them a principle of designation and election that had long been characteristic only of works that were referred to an ancient *auctoritas* and that had become part of a corpus of works continually cited and tirelessly commented upon.

By the same token, the radical reversal in the seventeenth or eighteenth century between the abandonment of the author-function among scientific texts and the demand for an author-function in poetic and fictional texts becomes somewhat less clear. If by twisting the rule of individual attribution of literary works the various games played with the author's name (dissimulation, disguise, usurpation) in reality confirmed the rule of the individual attribution of literary works,[48] it is less certain that a rule of anonymity commanded the production of scientific statements. For a notable length of time the validation of an experience or the accreditation of a proposition presupposed the guarantee provided by a proper name – the proper names of those who, by their position in society, had the power to proclaim the truth.[49] The fact that scholars and practitioners disappeared behind aristocratic authority in no way resulted in the anonymity of a discourse whose authenticity was not exclusively dependent on its compatibility with an already constituted body of knowledge. During the seventeenth and the eighteenth centuries a number of scientific texts displayed a characteristic that Foucault (perhaps wrongly) reserved to medieval works alone: later scientific texts were also 'accepted . . . and accepted as "true," only when marked with the name of their author' – an 'author', however, who was long understood as someone whose social position could lend 'authority' to intellectual discourse.

'What is an author?' The few reflections presented here are not intended as an answer to the question. All they hope to do is to stress that the history of the book, in all its various dimensions, can have some pertinence to the problem. It would be a mistake to reduce the construction of an author-function, understood as the major criterion for the attribution of texts, to oversimplified or too-univocal formulas. Nor can that construction be pinned down to one determining cause or a unique historical moment. The present text, which examines three sets of mechanisms – juridical, repressive,[50] and material – fundamental for the invention of the 'author', simply aims at staking out an area for possible future study. The author-function, inscribed in the books themselves, ordering all attempts to establish textual classifications commanding the rules for the publication of texts, is henceforth at the centre of all questions linking the study of the production, forms, and readers of texts.

3

Libraries without Walls

These examples made it possible for a librarian of genius to discover the fundamental law of the Library. This thinker observed that all the books, no matter how diverse they might be, are made up of the same elements: the space, the period, the comma, the twenty-two letters of the alphabet. He also alleged a fact which travelers have confirmed: *In the vast Library there are no two identical books.* From these two incontrovertible premises he deduced that the Library is total and that its shelves register all the possible combinations of the twenty-odd orthographical symbols (a number which, although vast, is not infinite): in other words, all that it is given to express, in all languages. Everything: the minutely detailed history of the future, the archangels' autobiographies, the faithful catalogue of the Library, thousands and thousands of false catalogues, the demonstration of the fallacy of those catalogues, the demonstration of the fallacy of the true catalogue, the Gnostic gospel of Basilides, the commentary on that gospel, the commentary on the commentary on that gospel, the true story of your death, the translation of all books in all languages, the interpolations of every book in all books. When it was proclaimed that the Library contained all books, the first impression was one of extravagant happiness.[1]

'When it was proclaimed that the Library contained all books, the first impression was one of extravagant happiness.' The dream of a library (in a variety of configurations) that would bring together all accumulated knowledge and all the books ever written can be found throughout the history of Western civilization. It underlay the constitution of great princely, ecclesiastical, and private 'libraries'; it justified a tenacious search for rare books, lost editions, and texts that had disappeared; it commanded architectural projects to construct edifices capable of welcoming the world's memory.

In 1785 Etienne-Louis Boullée proposed a project for the reconstruction of the Bibliothèque du Roi.[2] The architect's guiding idea was to cover the long (100 × 30 metres) interior court between the existing buildings with a barrel vault, thus making a reading room that would be the largest in all Europe. Along the sides of this 'immense basilica' lighted by a skylight at the top of the vault there were to be four stepped tiers lined with bookshelves, the uppermost of which provided a base for a colonnade. The colonnade was to be continued at either end of the room to form something like a 'triumphal arch' with the curve of the vault 'under which two allegorical statues could be put'. The works shelved in this reading room were to be placed within easy reach for readers who strolled before them, or they could be obtained by means of a human chain of 'persons placed on various levels and distributed so as to pass the books from hand to hand'.

In the perspective view that accompanied the *Mémoire* describing the project and in Boullée's presentation model tiny figures of readers draped in Roman togas are visible (one can count forty-four of them). They are walking among the books accumulated there; they pause, standing, to read a book, or they group around the few tables placed in the hall. The message is clear: a space in the form of a basilica and devoted to reading recuperates a sacred character that ecclesiastical buildings had lost; study is like a voyage among books punctuated by advances and halts, by solitary reading, and by erudite conversation.

The acknowledged model for Boullée's representation of his reading room is Raphael's *School of Athens*, but there are important difference between the two depictions. In the fresco in the Stanza della Segnatura there are few books, and the few that are shown are in the hands of the person who composed or copied them; in Boullée's drawing the thousands of books of the Bibliothèque du Roi constitute a universal body of knowledge that has been conserved and reduced to a thesaurus. Similarly, in Boullée's vision, the perspective is no longer structured to present an open porch, a human presence, and the power of creative discourse (that of Plato and of Aristotle surrounded by their disciples); rather it converges towards a door that marks the threshold between the profane world of the ignorant and the world of learning's elect and towards an allegorical statue in the classical mode, a symbol of the heritage that must be brought together and mastered before new thoughts are conceivable.

Bringing together the entire written patrimony of humanity in one place proves an impossible task, though. When print produced a proliferation of titles and editions, it ruined all hope for an exhaustive collection. Even for those who held that a library must be encyclopedic, selection was an absolute necessity. This was true for Gabriel Naudé in his *Advis pour dresser une Bibliothèque*, written in 1627 and addressed to Henri de Mesmes, *président* at the Parlement de Paris and a great book collector.[3] Against the model of the *cabinet curieux* or the *cabinet choisi* reserved to the delectation of their proprietor and gathering together a small number of books distinguished for their rarity or their luxury, Naudé pleads for a well-furnished library: 'It is much more useful and necessary to have, for example, a great quantity of books well bound in the ordinary fashion than to fill only some small, pale, gilded, and decorous room or cabinet enriched with all manner of little oddities [*mignardise*], luxuries, and superfluities.'[4] A library is not built to satisfy egotistical enjoyments but because there is 'no more honest and assured means for acquiring a great renown among the peoples than to erect handsome and magnificent Libraries in order then to dedicate and consecrate them to the use of the public'.[5] This noble design had a corollary:

> This is why I will always esteem that it is most appropriate to gather to that effect all sorts of Books (subject to the few precautions, however, that I shall state below), since a Library arranged for the use of the public must be universal, and it cannot be so if it does not contain all the principal Authors who have written on the great diversity of particular subjects.[6]

Ideally made up of an 'infinity of good, singular, and remarkable' works, the library must none the less limit its ambitions and make choices:

> Still, in order not to leave this quantity infinite by not defining it, and also in order not to throw the curious out of all hope of being able to accomplish and come to the end of this handsome enterprise, it seems to me that it is appropriate to do as the Physicians do, who order the quantity of drugs according to their quality, and to say

that one cannot lack gathering all those [books] that have the qualities and conditions required for being put in a Library.[7]

Naudé's *Advis* thus functons to guide the collector as he makes necessary selections and takes the appropriate 'precautions', since Naudé indicates the authors and the works absolutely indispensable for his library.

The division between the books that one absolutely must possess and those that might (or must) be left aside is only one of the ways to mitigate the problem of the impossibility of a universal library. There were other ways, which the language of the seventeenth and eighteenth centuries indicated with the very term defining the place in which the books were kept: *bibliothèque*. In the entry for that word in Furetière's *Dictionnaire* (1690) the first definition is the most traditional meaning: '*Bibliothèque*: Apartment or place destined for putting books; gallery, building full of books. Also said in general of the books that are placed in this vessel.' Next comes a second meaning designating a book rather than a place: '*Bibliothèque* is also a Collection, a Compilation of several works of the same nature or of Authors who have compiled all that can be [compiled] on the same subject.'

In his *Advis* Naudé praises the many merits of the collections that constitute as many 'libraries' in one work:

In the first place, they save us the trouble of seeking out an infinite number of highly rare and curious books; secondly, because they leave space for many others and give relief to a Library; thirdly, because they condense for us in one volume and commodiously what we would have to seek with much trouble in several places; and finally, because they bring with them a great saving, being certain that it requires fewer testons [coins worth ten sous] to buy them than it would require écus if one wanted to have separately all the [works] that they contain.[8]

The Latin terms for a collection vary considerably in these titles: *thesaurus, corpus, catalogus, flores*, and so forth. In French the genre was usually qualified as a *bibliothèque*. Four years after the publication of Furetière's *Dictionnaire*, the *Dictionnaire* of the Académie Française bore witness to this preference: 'One also calls *Bibliothèques* Collections and Compilations of works of like nature.' Three examples follow the definition: '*La Bibliothèque des Pères, La Nouvelle Bibliothèque des Pères, La Bibliothèque du Droit François.*'

Eighteenth-century bookseller-publishers published great numbers of these multiple-volume collections gathering together published works in a given genre such as novels, tales, or travel accounts. Not all such collections bore the name *bibliothèque*. For example, there was the sixteen-volume *Histoire générale des voyages* of Abbé Prévost covering the years from 1746 to 1761, published first in quarto format and later, between 1746 and 1789, in eighty duodecimo volumes; there were two publications put out by Charles Garnier, the *Cabinet des fées* (1785–9), forty-one volumes in octavo format, and the *Voyages imaginaires, songes, visions et romans cabalistiques* (1787–9), in thirty-nine octavo sized volumes. Many collections, however, made use of both the formula and the term inaugurated by the Amsterdam periodicals of Jean Le Clerc, the *Bibliothèque universelle et historique (1686–93),* the *Bibliothèque choisie* (1703–13), and the *Bibliothèque ancienne et moderne: Pour servir de suite aux Bibliothèques universelle et choisie* (1714–27). In all, there were thirty-one periodical publications in the French language, some of which lasted longer than others, that were offered under the title of *bibliothèque* between 1686 and 1789.[9] The term was used throughout the century, with seventeen titles published before 1750 and fourteen after. Several of these publications were not periodicals, properly speaking, but imposing collections of texts related by their genre or their targeted audience. One such was the *Bibliothèque universelle des romans* (Paris, 1775–89, 224 volumes in duodecimo format), which was presented as a 'periodical work in which is given the reasoned analysis of Novels ancient and modern, French or translated into our language', which published extracts and summaries, historical and critical notes, unabridged texts of novels, and tales both ancient and original.[10] Another was the *Bibliothèque universelle des dames* (Paris, 1785–97, 156 octodecimo-sized volumes), which had encyclopedic ambitions, given that it contained travel narratives, novels, and works of history, morality, mathematics and astronomy, physics and natural history, and all the liberal arts.

These imposing 'libraries', along with the encyclopedias and the dictionaries, constituted a major part of the great publishing ventures of the eighteenth century. As Louis-Sébastien Mercier noted, they guaranteed the diffusion of knowledge – or at least of literary pleasure – and they provided a living for a multitude of the people who were scornfully called *demi-littérateurs* or *écrivailleurs*. As Mercier put it:

> Panckoucke and Vincent commision [dictionaries] from any compiler armed with scribes; volumes are built by the alphabet just as an edifice is constructed in the space of so many months. The [success of the] work is sure thanks to maneuvers. Everything has been put in dictionaries. The

scholars complain: they are wrong. Must not science descend to all conditions?[11]

The 'libraries', which aimed at being exhaustive and universal in any given genre or domain, had a counterpoint in the eighteenth century in a vast number of equally popular small, concise, and easily handled volumes named *extraits, esprits, abrégés, analyses,* and so forth.[12]

The smaller, portable anthologies were another form of 'library' produced by the book trade. Even if both genres offered extracts, their intention was not the same. The smaller works aimed at eliminating, selecting, and reducing rather than accumulating a multitude of separate and dispersed works in one collection (periodical or not). If the way in which collections in the form of a *bibliothèque* were constructed aimed at accomplishing as best one could the impossible task of gathering together for every reader all the books concerning a particular sphere, an appeal to analysis and esprit implied that such a task was useless or harmful, and that the necessary knowledge, available in a small number of works, needed to be concentrated or distilled like a chemical substance. In that belief they agreed with the utopias of the century that rejected the encyclopedic libraries as over-encumbered and superfluous and permitted only a very few books in their ideal library.

In his utopia (more accurately, his uchronia) of 1771, *L'An 2440,* Louis-Sébastien Mercier pays a visit to the library of the king and finds it to be somewhat singular: 'In place of those four galleries of immense length, which contained many thousands of volumes, I could find only one small cabinet, in which were several books that seemed to me far from voluminous.' Intrigued, Mercier asks the librarian what has happened, and the librarian answers that before burning all the books judged to be 'either frivolous or useless or dangerous', the enlightened men of the twenty-fifth century saved the essential, which took up little room:

> As we are neither unjust nor like the Saracens, who heated their baths with masterworks, we made a choice: wise men extracted the substance from a thousand in-folio volumes, all of which they transferred into a small duodecimo-sized volume, somewhat in the same way that the skilful chemists who extract the virtue from plants concentrate it in a flask and throw out the vulgar liquors. We have abridged what seemed of most importance; the best have been reprinted; and all the whole corrected according to the true principles of morality. Our compilers are estimable people and dear to the nation; they had taste, and as they were in a creative frame of mind, they were able to choose what was excellent and reject what was not.[13]

The tension between comprehensiveness and essence thus ordered the complex and contradictory relations between the library in its usual spatial and architectural sense and print genres (only some of which were called *bibliothèques*) – relationships that assigned to the 'library' as a book, be it one volume or one of a series, the functions of accumulation or of selection attributed to the place.[14]

But a library was not only a place or a collection. Furetière's *Dictionnaire* proposes a third definition of the term (not found in the more concise entry of the *Dictionnaire* of the Académie): 'One also calls *Bibliothèque* the books that contain the Catalogues of the books in the *Bibliothèques*. Gesner, Possevin, Photius, have made *Bibliothèques*. . . . Father Labbé, a Jesuit, has made the *Bibliothèque des Bibliothèques* in an octavo-sized book that contains only the catalogue of the names of those who have written *Bibliothèques*.'[15] For anyone who might wish to design an open and universal library, the possession of such catalogues was a necessity. The sum of their titles defined an ideal library freed from the constraints imposed by any one actual collection and overflowing the limits inherent in anthologies and compilations by the immaterial construction of a sort of library of all libraries in which nothing (or almost nothing) was lacking. Naudé tells his interlocutor that the accumulation and copying of catalogues of libraries is obligatory: 'One must not omit nor neglect to have transcribed all the Catalogues, not only of the great and renowned Libraries, ancient or modern, public or private, in the possession of our compatriots or of foreigners, but also the Studies and Cabinets that for not being known or frequented remain buried in a perpetual silence.' Naudé gives as one of his reasons for this requirement: 'It is to do pleasure and service to a friend, when one cannot furnish him with the book he lacks, to show and designate to him the place where he truly can find a copy of it, as one can easily do by means of these Catalogues.'[16] Thanks to the circulation of the catalogues, the closed world of individual libraries could be transformed into an infinite universe of books noted, reviewed, visited, consulted and, eventually, borrowed.

Furetière's definition slips from catalogues of particular holdings towards another sort of work. A 'library' is not only the inventory of the books assembled in a specific place; it can be an inventory of all the books ever written on a given subject or by all the authors of a given nation. Thus Furetière notes: 'In France, there is not yet a general *Bibliothèque* of all the Authors. There are particular ones by the Sieur La Croix du Maine Manceau and Anthoine

Du Verdier. Spain has one by Nicolas Anthonio. There is also a *Bibliothèque d'Espagne* of Peregrinus, and the *Bibliothèque des Escrivains Espagnols* by André Schot in 1608.'[17] Thus the genre that the *Dictionnaire* evokes and designates with the term *bibliothèque* is defined according to two criteria: it lists authors; it respects the national framework (France, Spain).

At the end of the seventeenth century such 'libraries' already had a long history.[18] Three such works had appeared before 1550, the *Cathalogus illustrium virorum Germaniae suis ingeniis et lucubrationibus omnifariam exornantium* of Johann Tritheim (Mainz, 1495), the *Bibliotheca Universalis, sive Catalogus omnium scriptorum locupletissimus, in tribus linguis, Latina, Graeca, et Hebraica* of Conrad Gesner (Zurich, 1545), and the *Illustrium Maioris Britanniae Scriptorum* of John Bale (Ipswich, 1548). These three works have several traits in common: they are written in Latin, they list for the most part ancient authors, and they privilege works written in the classical languages. Beyond these similarities, their choices varied. First, as to the framework chosen: a national territory (*Germania* for Tritheim and Great Britain for Bale, who restricts the scope of his work in its full title: *Illustrium Maioris Britanniae Scriptorum, Hoc Est Angliae, Cambriae, ac Scotiae Summarium*); the whole of humanity for Gesner. Next, as to the name of the work: Tritheim and Bale (in a new edition of his work in 1557) use the term *catalogus*, but Gesner innovates, launching a new usage of *bibliotheca* that detaches the word from its material definition and invests the library without walls proposed in his book with universality. Finally, the three works differ in their organization: Tritheim and Bale chose a chronological structure (the latter specifying *in quasdam centurias divisum cum diversitate doctrinarum atque; annorum recta supputatione per omnes aetates a Iapheto sanctissimi Noah filio, ad annum domini M.D. XLVIII*), providing an alphabetical index to make the work easier to consult. Once again Gesner stands alone, opting for alphabetical order but in the medieval style (unlike Tritheim and Bale) and classifying his authors by their baptismal names – that is, their first names. The declared universality of his *Bibliotheca* presupposes an exhaustive survey that retains ancients and contemporaries, printed texts and manuscript texts, learned authors and less learned authors. The long title justifies the dual usefulness of the book – *Opus novum, et non Bibliothecis tantum publicis privatisque instituendis necessarium, sed studiosis omnibus cuiuscunque artis aut scientiae ad studia melius formanda utilissimum* – after having declared its content – *Catalogus omnium scriptorum locupletissimus, in tribus linguis, Latina, Graeca, et Hebraica: extantium et non extantium, veterum et recentiorum in hunc usque diem, doctorum et non doctorum, publicatorum et in Bibliothecis latentium.*[19]

When Anton Francesco Doni published his *Libraria . . . Nella quale sono scritti tutti gl'Autori vulgari con cento discorsi sopra quelli: Tutte le tradutioni fatte dell'altre lingue, nella nostra e una tavola generalmente come si costuma fra Librari* (Gabriele Giolito de' Ferrari, Venice, 1550), he inaugurated a new mode of presentation in this genre.[20] He innovated in three ways: first, in language, since the *Libraria* reviewed only authors or translators in the vernacular and is itself written in the vulgar tongue. Next, the intention of the book was new: it contains no inventory of all authors, no collection of judgements; rather, it is primarily designed to provide information on titles available in the vernacular: 'I have made this library only to give knowledge of all the books printed in the vulgar language so that people who like to read in our language may know how many works have been published and what [they are], not to judge which are good and which bad.' The third novelty lay in the work's format. Doni abandons large formats (the quarto of Tritheim and Bale, the in-folio of Gesner) to publish his *Libraria* in a more manageable duodecimo format that the reader who haunted the bookshops in search of the titles that this ideal library (again, without walls) might suggest could easily carry.

The small volume of the *Libraria* published in 1550 had 144 pages, and it mentioned 159 authors, arranged in alphabetical order by their first names (from Acarisio da Cento to Vincenzo Rinchiera). Doni plays learned games with the fourteen letters of the alphabet around which his nomenclature is organized. The initial of the given name of the authors listed in a section was also the initial of the given name of the dedicatee mentioned in a preamble heading the section, as well as the initial of the first word in that brief text (for example, the 'A' section was headed, 'Abate Abati. Assai son l'opere . . .'). After this list of all the authors who had published in the vulgar tongue, Doni provides three other lists: a typology of vernacular genres ('Humanità / Dialoghi / Comedie / Rime / Lettere / Romanzi / Storie'), an inventory of texts translated from Latin into Italian (arranged according to another system as 'Sacra Scrittura et Spirituali / Historie / Epistole tradotte / Comedie Tragedie / Medicina'), and a 'Tavola Generale di tutti libri volgari' in the form of a bookseller's catlogue but without bibliographic information on specific editions.

A year after this first book Doni published *La Seconda Libraria* listing texts that had not yet been printed. The principle in this work was the same as in the first, with an alphabetical inventory from Acarisio da Cento to Zanobi

Fiorentino and with a similar game of correspondences between the letter of the alphabet pertaining to each section and the initial letter of the first word of the brief tales or apologues that opened each section. As Amedeo Quondam has noted, the *Libraria* of manuscript works – 'of Books that the Author has seen in manuscript and which are not yet printed' – is largely fictional, enumerating invented authors and imaginary titles. It provides something like a 'paradoxical and ironic double' to the *Libraria* that surveys published works.[21] In 1557 Doni joined together his two 'libraries' and published them in an octavo-sized volume printed in Venice by Gabriele Giolito de' Ferrari. He added to them a third treatise that amplified a text known as early as 1551 on 'the foundation of the Academies, together with their names, their mottoes, their emblems, and the works produced by all the Academicians'. Defined on the 1557 title page as a 'Book necessary and useful to all those who have a need to know the language and who wish to know how to write and to reason about all the authors, books, and works', Doni's two *librarie* form a complex book. Their bibliographic definition ('they were not only the first Italian national bibliographies; they were also the first bibliographies in a vulgar tongue')[22] fails to do justice to their multiple significance: they proclaim the excellence and the dignity conquered by the vulgar language; they constitute a repertory of contemporary authors; they dismantle, in a parodic key, the recipes for literary invention.

Doni's work was known in France, where it gave direct inspiration to the two 'libraries' encountered in chapter 2, the one published in 1584 by François de La Croix du Maine and the other published in 1585 by Antoine Du Verdier.[23] These two works share an interest in demonstrating the superiority of the French language over the Italian language by citing the number of authors who wrote in the vernacular, by the fact that French had been used as a literary language longer than Italian, and by the scope of the learning of French expression. This intention is explicit in the *Premier volume de la Bibliothèque du Sieur de La Croix du Maine. Qui est un catalogue général de toutes sortes d'Autheurs, qui ont escrit en François depuis cinq cents ans et plus, jusques à ce jourd'huy* (Abel L'Angelier, Paris, 1584). Not only does La Croix du Maine insist in his title on the length of time during which the French language had been used ('for five hundred years and more'), he also compares, to the advantage of France, the 'three thousand authors' (in fact 2,031) inventoried in his 'catalogue' and the three hundred (in fact 159) who figured in Doni's *Libraria*, a fact to which, he adds, 'all can testify with me who have read the book of Antoine-François Dony Florentine, who brought into the light a work of his that he called the Library – that is, the Catalogue of Italian books ancient and modern – that he had printed four years ago, to wit, in the year of salvation 1580' (La Croix du Maine here takes one of the later editions of Doni's work for its first edition, which was published some thirty years earlier).

In *La Bibliothèque d'Antoine Du Verdier, Seigneur de Vauprivas: Contenant le Catalogue de tous ceux qui ont escrit, ou traduict in François, et autres Dialectes de ce Royaume* (Lyons: Barthélémy Honorat, 1585) recognition of the superiority of France does not refer explicitly to Italy: 'In short, excellent Writers and truly good books have so multiplied that it seems now that we have no more need to borrow any knowledge from others, having all sciences among us, perhaps in better form, at least better to our taste and easier for us to learn.' The model from which Du Verdier took inspiration was not Doni but Gesner: 'In our times Conrad Gesner has gathered together all Authors whatsoever in three languages, Hebraic, Greek, and Latin, to his great honour and the common benefit.' It was in reference to that ancient knowledge and that great example ('I have given my book the title of *Bibliothèque* because Gesner thus entitled his own') that Du Verdier constructed the catalogue by which he intended to prove the excellence of the moderns: 'I have worked to do the like for our French people who have written in our language in order to show the world to what extent our country is abundant in good minds.' Unlike La Croix du Maine, Du Verdier feels no need to call on the great antiquity of the use of the French language; he simply surveys modern authors 'from sixty or seventy years past', whom he finds sufficiently numerous and excellent to obviate any need to name older writers, since before that time 'our [authors] were somewhat heavy in their writings.'

There are obvious similarities between Doni's *Libraria* and La Croix du Maine's *Bibliothèque*: both inventory books (both printed and manuscript) written or translated into the vulgar tongue; both offer brief biographies of some of the authors whose works they list (La Croix du Maine says in his subtitle, 'with a Discourse on the lives of the most illustrious and renowned among the three thousand who are included in this work, together with a relation of their compositions both printed and other'); both classify authors in strict alphabetical order by author's given name (from Abel Foulon to Yves Le Fortier for La Croix du Maine). In dedicating his work to the king (Henri III), La Croix du Maine thought it necessary to justify this arrangement that overlooked differences in social condition:

There remains one point to note to you, Lord of France, which is that you must not judge it ill if I have put the names of some poeple into an order about which (according to some hasty judgements) you might say that I had erred by doing so, and [that you will acknowledge] that I was not too wrong in this case. As, for example, if you see that I have spoken of the Kings of France, whether of François I, Charles IX, or Henri III, would you say that I was mistaken when I happened to place them after their subjects, or else having spoken of the father or the mother when I have put the children first, or disciples before their masters? Certainly I have felt the impropriety of having thus observed an alphabetical or A, B, C order, but I have done so everywhere where it is called for, in order to avoid all calumny and to remain in amity with everyone.

There are none the less fundamental differences between the works of Doni and La Croix du Maine that come from their quite different manner of understanding the library without walls. First, there is a physical and formal difference between the two works: far from being a manageable small-format book in the manner of the *Libraria*, La Croix du Maine's *Bibliothèque* was a majestic folio volume, a *libro da banco*, to use Armando Petrucci's terminology, not a *libro da bisaccia* (saddlebag book) or a *libretto da mano* (little handbook).[24] The world referred to in La Croix du Maine's *Bibliothèque* is not the book trade and its commerce but the world of the *cabinet* (book room), of study, and of compilation. In a short piece entitled *Desseins, ou Projects du Sieur de La Croix du Maine, presentez au Trèschrestien Roy de France et de Pologne Henri III du nom, l'an 1583, au mois de May* La Croix du Maine declared that he owns in his library 'eight hundred volumes of Memoirs and diverse Collections, written by my hand and otherwise, and all of my invention or sought by myself, and extracts from all the books that I have read until this day, of which the number is infinite, as can easily be seen by the twenty-five or thirty thousand notebooks and chapters on all sorts of subjects that can fall within man's ken'. Anton Francesco Doni's *Libraria* was founded on the practice of literary novelties; La Croix du Maine's *Bibliothèque* was based on the scholastic tradition of commonplace books. A literate man without originality, but not without prolixity since he claims to have composed several hundred works (which he enumerates in a *Discours du Sieur de La Croix du Maine contenant sommairement les Noms, Tiltres et Inscriptions de la plus grande partie de ses Oeuvres Latines et Françoises* dated 1579), La Croix du Maine scrupulously calculates his compilation activities. He states that he wrote three hours per day, and he figures that if in one hour he filled one sheet of paper of over one hundred lines, his yearly production was some one thousand sheets. None of the works that he wrote in this manner was published (with the exception of the *Premier Volume de la Bibliothèque*), which means that it is difficult to evaluate the results of his assiduous labours. It is certain, however, that his work was organized intellectually according to the principle of the notebook or the commonplace book and that it gathered under one heading extracts from various authors' works. Hence the central importance that La Croix du Maine gives to the instruments for putting order into this proliferating material, the 'three hundred tables of commonplaces that I have made to clarify my purpose ... inasmuch as these tables serve as a key to explain what I have written in entire articles'.

La Croix du Maine's work also differed from Doni's in that the *Premier Volume* of his *Bibliothèque* was 'dedicated and presented to the King', whose engraved portrait figured on the page facing the dedication addressed to him. In both the *Desseins, ou Projects* of 1583 and the *Premier Volume de la Bibliothèque* published the following year La Croix du Maine pursued the same aim of obtaining the sovereign's protection, which had a cash value in terms of gratifications and posts. The proposition that he submitted in 1583 fitted into this logic of monarchical patronage. It provides a plan

> to erect a Library, perfect and accomplished in all points, if it please his Majesty to accept it and to furnish the Books, Memoirs, or Collections to fill the one hundred Bookcases whose form or fashion is represented here: each of these containing one hundred volumes, which in all number ten thousand, divided into Books, Chapters, Notebooks, and commonplaces, and further reduced to order of A, B, C in order to locate them more easily.

The originality of this 'notice to erect a library', which preceded Naudé's project by a half century, lay in La Croix du Maine's desire to embody the immaterial and universal library of *loci communes* in a real library, one of whose bookcases (one of the *cent Buffets*) is figured on one page of the work. He was less interested in accumulating books than in gathering under the one hundred (actually 108) topics that corrresponded to as many *buffets* works in various forms (printed books but also memoirs and manuscript compilations): 'all that can be found in writing touching that chosen matter . . . reduced to such a number and such an order that it will be quite difficult to find anything to change in it.' Secure in his experience and his manuscripts, La Croix du Maine claimed that he could bring together in eight or fifteen days the works needed to fill any one of the one hundred (or 108) *buffets*.

Thus it was on the basis of the practice of the commonplace book that the totally original system of classification proposed by La Croix du Maine should be understood.[25] The work was divided into seven 'orders': 'sacred things', 'arts and sciences', 'description of the Universe both in general and in particular', 'the human race', 'famous men in War', 'the works of God', and 'miscellanies of various Memoirs', subdivided into a total of 108 'classes'. Unlike the twenty-one categories in Gesner's *Pandectarum sive Partitionum, universalium . . . libri XXI* (Zurich, 1548), this organization was not intended to construct a tree of knowledge that proceeded by successive divisions. In Gesner's work, the *artes et scientia* that make up *philosophia* are divided into *substantiales* (subdivided into *physica* or *naturali philosophia, metaphysica et theologia gentilium, ethica* or *morali philosophia, oeconomica, politica, jurisprudentia, medicina, theologia christiana*) and *praeparantes.* The latter category is subdivided into *ornantes* (*historia, geographia, divinatio et magia,* and *artes illiteratae et mechanicae*) and *necessariae.* The latter are subdivided into *mathematicae* (*arithmetica, geometria, musica, astronomia,* and *astrologia*) and *sermocinales,* which were *grammatica et philologia, dialectica, rhetorica,* and *poetica.* A 'Tabula de singulis pandectarum libris' arranges the various bibliographical classes according to a systematic order, the order of the divisions of *philosophia,* understood as a trajectory of knowledge leading from the *trivium* and the *quadrivium* to Christian theology. There is none of this in the taxonomy proposed by La Croix du Maine, which has no overall governing system, but simply juxtaposes convenient headings in view of gathering together extracts and commonplaces. The fourth 'order', for example, includes the bookcases devoted to 'Man and what is dependent on him', 'Diseases of Men and their remedies', 'Illustrious and other Women', 'Worldly Wisdom, or Instruction for men', 'Divers exercises of Nobles and Gentlemen', 'Miscellaneous exercises for the mind or the body', 'Divers traffics and commerce of men on sea and on land', 'Divers customs and fashions of living everywhere in the universe', 'Men of honest exercise', and 'Officers of long robe, or of the Judiciary'.

Because it was to be an example worthy of being imitated, the 'perfect and accomplished' library set up by the king was to be 'the means for rendering the less learned or the totally ignorant well informed and knowledgeable, and also to make the vice-ridden exercise virtue if they conform to their Prince'. Similarly, only the approval of the king could give authority to the *Premier Volume de la Bibliothèque* published in 1584 and to all the other books that were supposed to follow it. At the end of his dedicatory epistle, signed 'FRANÇOIS DE LA CROIX DV MAINE, the anagram for which is RACE DV MANS, SI FIDEL' A SON ROY', La Croix du Maine suggests a more concrete version of the connection with the sovereign: 'If your Majesty should desire to know what are the other [volumes] that I have written and composed for the ornamentation and illustration of your so famous and flourishing Kingdom, I am ready to provide a reading (when it may please you to so command me) of the Discourse that I had printed five years ago touching the general catalogue of my works.' Doni's *Libraria* had multiple dedicatees (one for each letter of the alphabet) and was aimed at a broader audience. La Croix du Maine's *Bibliothèque* supposes an exclusive relationship, established in proximity by reading aloud, between an author in search of protection and the monarch whose patronage he seeks.

A final difference between Doni's work and that of La Croix du Maine is that the Florentine's work was solidly connected with publishing activities; it was 'constructed in direct contact with (and probably backed by) two of the publishers of greatest cultural importance in the mid-sixteenth century', the Venetians Gabriele Giolito de' Ferrari, the publisher of the first edition and of the complete edition of the work, and Francesco Marcolini, the publisher of the *Seconda Libraria*.[26] La Croix du Maine's work originated in the construction of his private library, begun in his university years. That was the collection of printed books and manuscript memoirs that La Croix du Maine had transported to Paris in 1582:

> I will say that after having been thirteen or fourteen years writing, collecting, and seeking Memoirs everywhere, and finally seeing that I had a good many (to the number of seven or eight hundred volumes) I decided to make my home in Paris and, to that effect, I had three wagons loaded with my volumes and Memoirs and with books, both written by hand and otherwise, taken there, and I arrived in Paris on the last day of May in the year 1582.

The library that La Croix du Maine gathered together and, in part, produced provided support for all his undertakings. For one thing, it was something like a prefiguration of the hundred-bookcase library that he proposed to the king (which was what led him to state that 'the most difficult part of the enterprise is done'). For another, his library formed the matrix of all the ideal libraries that he was to imagine. The library published in 1584 was in fact little more than an *Epitomé* of a more ambitious undertaking, the projected *Grande Bibliothèque Françoise* (and its twin, a *Bibliothèque Latine*). In these two works (never published) the authors' names were to be accompanied by information on editions, dedicatees, and the texts:

> I was not content to have put in those Latin and French Libraries the catalogue of the works or writings of each author, but beyond that I included by whom they were printed, in what size or format, in what year, how many pages they contained, and above all the name of those men or women to whom they were dedicated, without omitting their full and entire qualities. Aside from that, I put in the beginning or first line of their work and composition and in what age their authors lived.

Imitating Gesner, La Croix du Maine added to his *Bibliothèques* volumes of *Pandectes Latines et Françoises* ('to wit, a very ample Catalogue of all the Authors who have written in each art, science or profession of studies, which I have divided according to the seven arts that we call liberal') and several volumes of what he called a *mentionnaire*, 'which is like a book of commonplaces, or an Aggregation of authors who have made mention of particular things'. Claiming to have scrutinized the works of 'ten thousand authors', La Croix du Maine notes that in these *mentionnaires* (also unpublished) he 'quotes passages of the said authors further observing and noting in what book, what chapter or what article, on what leaf, even on what page or side can be found what I have read, and in what size is the book, and of what printing'.

Three different principles of classification exist concurrently in La Croix du Maine's works. The first organizing criterion is the category of the author. The author-function, as Foucault defines it, is already sketched out here.[27] In the one published volume as in his *Grande Bibliothèque*, La Croix du Maine makes this the basic criterion for assigning discourses, which are organized alphabetically by their authors' given names. In announcing that he will provide authors' 'lives' (written, La Croix du Maine tells us, in imitation of Suetonius, Plutarch, and Paolo Giovio), he equates men of letters with military leaders, famous for their exploits, and with princes and grandees, masters of their deeds.

None the less, this first scheme for assigning works did not neglect the power of patronage. La Croix du Maine demonstrates this when he promises to note, for all the works mentioned in his unpublished *Grande Bibliothèque*, '*above all* [emphasis mine] the name of those men and women to whom they were dedicated, without omitting their full and entire qualities'. A work thus belongs as much to the person to whom it has been dedicated as it does to the person who has written it and, in the ideal library as on the title page, the two names of the author and the patron stood as proof of this.

A third criterion for classifying works eliminates assignment to an individual in favour of placing each work within an order or class of knowledge. It is the tension between the name and the commonplace that underlies Gesner's dual enterprise, the *Bibliotheca universalis* of 1545 and the *Pandectarum . . . libri XXI* three years later – a work that was presented as 'Secondus hic Bibliothecae nostrae Tomus est, totius philosophiae et omnium bonarum artium atque studiorum Locos communes et Ordines universales simul et particulares complectens.' That same tension is reflected in La Croix du Maine's bibliographic zeal, even though his grandiose projects were never realized.

The almost simultaneous publication of the two *Bibliothèques* (May 1584 for La Croix du Maine; 1585, with an end printing date of 15 December 1584 for Du Verdier) raises a problem. La Croix du Maine took the initiative and parried any possible accusation that he had plagiarized a work that had not yet been published but whose publication he knew was imminent, as proved by the entry under 'Antoine du Verdier' in the *Premier Volume de la Bibliothèque*: 'I have been assured that he is about to have printed a *Bibliothèque Françoise* of his own, of which I am not jealous.' Declaring furthermore that he never knew of the existence of Du Verdier's work, La Croix du Maine claims anteriority for his own venture, begun more than fifteen years before, and stresses the great distance ('more than a hundred leagues') that separated their places of residence, Paris and Lyons, where Du Verdier had settled in 1580. For good measure, La Croix du Maine states his scorn of plagiarism: 'I will confess to having undertaken to write a book against such kinds of people, usurpers taking credit for the work of others, which work I have entitled "The Rod, or the Scourge of Plagiarists", or of those who attribute to themselves and put under their own names works or compositions of which they are not the authors or inventors.' Furthermore, he founds the authority of his own book on the resources of his library and on his own knowledge: 'As for the authors I have mentioned in my work, I have seen or read them, and have them still before me for the most part without having borrowed them, for I will firmly say that I have never owed any Bookseller for books, and I have spent more than ten thousand livres in the fifteen or sixteen years since I began to love letters.' As in the travel narrations of the age, *auto-psie* – the action of seeing with one's own eyes ('I have seen them') – became the exclusive guarantee of truth. That certification of authenticity by direct experience is not without paradox in an author who compiles extracts and commonplaces in innumerable notebooks that he then presents as learning itself.

Du Verdier (who was first a financial officer in the *élection* of Forez, then contrôleur général des finances in Lyons),[28] weighed heavier in the social scales than La Croix du Maine, a simple provincial gentleman who had moved to Paris. Du Verdier's response was two-pronged: first, he mocked the erudite fanfaronades of his rival and expressed doubts about the existence of the many works La Croix du Maine promised:

> Someone (whose name I will not mention) who has sent me a great notebook and inventory of the books that he says he has composed before he was yet twenty years old [the catalogue of his works that La Croix du Maine had printed in 1579], which have surpassed five hundred volumes in number, decorated with the handsomest titles that one could imagine and which contain more than one hundred pages – a ridiculous and unbelievable, if not impossible, thing.

Furthermore, after Du Verdier had a look at the work in question (which he lists as being printed in Paris in his entry 'François de La Croix du Maine' in his own *Bibliothèque*), he questions the accuracy of the information given by La Croix du Maine because he surveys fictitious or unproductive authors and includes in his work 'several [authors] that never were in nature, or if they were, have written nothing, as he himself confesses'.

In its format (a heavy folio volume) and in its form (organized alphabetically by name), Antoine Du Verdier's *Bibliothèque* was akin to La Croix du Maine's work, but it is constructed on a different principle. Du Verdier's imagined library is not directly dependent upon the constitution of the author's own collection but is rather a conceptual entity detached from any particular material presence. Du Verdier's catalogue is indeed a 'library', but it is an all-inclusive library: 'As in the Library divers books are organized, where they are kept as if in their proper place, thus as many divers Authors and books are here put in such an order that at first sight one can locate them in their place and thus remember them.' In this exhaustive inventory every reader must be able to find what he or she needed and use that information to construct a library made up of real books.

It was in order to facilitate that task that Antoine Du Verdier gave the bibliographic information that was lacking in the *Epitomé* published by La Croix du Maine. As the title states, the work promises 'the place, form, name, and date, where, how, and by whom [the works listed] were brought to light [that is, printed]'. There was thus no contradiction between the design of a 'universal library of French books', which necessarily had no physical reality, and the making of a bibliographic instrument useful to all those who might want to create a collection. In parallel fashion, the attempt to be complete that led Du Verdier to mention Lutheran and Calvinist authors who wrote in French led to another aim: to make sure that 'Catholics are warned which books are reproved and censured so that they will flee them'. Whatever Du Verdier's own religious sentiments may have been, his *Bibliothèque* is thus explicitly invested with the same function as the catalogues of censured books put out by the Faculty of Theology of Paris, whose Index was first published in 1544, also using authors' names listed in alphabetical order (of family names, however) as the primary criterion for classifying titles.[29]

The various meanings given to the term for a library thus clearly show one of the major tensions that inhabited the literate of the early modern age and caused them anxiety. A universal library (or at least universal in one order of knowledge) could not be other than fictive, reduced to the dimensions of a catalogue, a nomenclature, or a survey. Conversely, any library that is actually installed in a specific place and that is made up of real works available for consultation and reading, no matter how rich it might be, gives only a truncated image of all accumulable knowledge. The irreducible gap between ideally exhaustive inventories and necessarily incomplete collections was experienced with intense frustration. It led to extravagant ventures assembling – in spirit, if not in reality – all possible books, all discoverable titles, all works ever written. 'When it was proclaimed that the Library contained all books, the first impression was one of extravagant happiness.'

Epilogue

—

As the twentieth century wanes, our dream is to be able to surmount the contradiction that long haunted Western Europeans' relationship with the book. The library of the future seems indeed to be in a sense a library without walls, as were the libraries that Gesner, Doni, and La Croix du Maine erected on paper. Unlike their catalogues, which furnished authors' names, the titles of works, and at times summaries of or extracts from the works, the library of the future is inscribed where all texts can be summoned, assembled, and read: on a screen. In the universe of remote communications made possible by computerized texts and electronic diffusion, texts are no longer prisoners of their original physical, material existence. Separated from the objects on which we are used to finding them, texts can be transmitted in a new form; there is no longer a necessary connection between where they are conserved and where they are read. The opposition long held to be insurmountable between the closed world of any finite collection, no matter what its size, and the infinite universe of all texts ever written is thus theoretically annihilated: now the catalogue of all catalogues ideally listing the totality of written production can be realized in a universal access to texts available for consultation at the reader's location.

This projection towards the future, written here in the present tense, retains something of the basically contradictory utopias proposed by Louis-Sébastien Mercier and Etienne Boullée. Still, it is perhaps not too soon to reflect on the effects of the change that it thus promises and announces. If texts are emancipated from the form that has conveyed them since the first centuries of the Christian era – the *codex*, the book composed of quires from which all printed objects with which we are familiar derive – by the same token all intellectual technologies and all the operations at work in the production of meaning will be modified. 'Forms effect meanings', D. F. McKenzie reminds us,[1] and his lesson, which should be taken to heart, warns us to be on guard against the illusion that wrongly reduces texts to their semantic content. When it passes from the *codex* to the monitor screen the 'same' text is no longer truly the same because the new formal devices that offer it to its reader modify the conditions of its reception and its comprehension.

When the text is carried by a new technique and embodied in a new physical form, it can be offered to manipulation by a reader who is no longer limited, as with the printed book, to adding hand-written matter in the spaces left blank in typographic composition and in binding.[2] At the same time, the end of the *codex* will signify the loss of acts and representations indissolubly linked to the book as we now know it. In the form that it has acquired in Western Europe since the beginning of the Christian era, the book has been one of the most powerful metaphors used for conceiving of the cosmos, nature, history, and the human body.³ If the object that has furnished the matrix of this repertory of images (poetic, philosophical, scientific) should disappear, the references and the procedures that organize the 'readability' of the physical world, equated with a book in *codex* form, would be profoundly upset as well.

Realizing the dream of the Renaissance bibliographers of making the particular place in which the reader finds himself or herself coincide perfectly with universal knowledge, thus putting that knowledge within grasp, inevitably presupposes a new definition of the concept of the text, wrenched away from its immediate association (so evident to us) with the specific form of the book – the *codex* – that some seventeen or eighteen centuries ago replaced another form, the *volumen* or roll.⁴ The historian's musings proposed in the present work thus lead to a question essential in our own present time – not the overworked question of the supposed disappearance of writing, which is more resistant than has been thought, but the question of a possible revolution in the forms of its dissemination and appropriation.

Notes

Chapter 1   Communities of Readers

This chapter is dedicated to the memory of Michel de Certeau.

1 Michel de Certeau, *L'invention du quotidien*, vol. 1, *Arts de faire* (1980), new edn, ed. Luce Giard (Gallimard, Paris, 1990), p. 251, quoted from Certeau, *The Practice of Everyday Life*, tr. Steven F. Rendall (University of California Press, Berkeley, Los Angeles, and London, 1984), p. 174.

2 Certeau, *L'invention du quotidien*, p. 247, quoted from *The Practice of Everyday Life*, pp. 170–1. On the coupling of reading and writing in Certeau, see Anne-Marie Chartier and Jean Hébrard, *'L'invention du quotidien*, une lecture, des usages', *Le débat*, 49 (March–April 1988), pp. 97–108.

3 Paul Ricoeur, *Temps et récit*, 3 vols (Editions du Seuil, Paris, 1985), vol. 3, *Le temps raconté*, pp. 228–63, available in English as Ricoeur, *Time and Narrative*, tr. Kathleen McLaughlin and David Pellauer, 3 vols (University of Chicago Press, Chicago, 1984–8).

4 Michel de Certeau, 'La lecture absolue (Théorie et pratique des mystiques chrétiens: XVIe–XVIIe siècles)', in *Problèmes actuels de la lecture*, ed. Lucien Dällenbach and Jean Ricardou (Editions Clancier-Guénaud, Paris, 1982), pp. 65–79,

quotation p. 67. The suggestions in this essay also appear in Michel de Certeau, *La fable mystique: XVIe–XVIIe siècle* (Gallimard, Paris, 1982, 1987), esp. in pt 3, 'La scène de l'énonciation', pp. 209–73, available in English as Certeau, *The Mystic Fable: The Sixteenth and Seventeenth Centuries*, tr. Michael B. Smith (University of Chicago Press, Chicago, 1992).

5 For one example of such an approach, see Lisa Jardine and Anthony Grafton, '"Studied for Action": How Gabriel Harvey Read His Livy', *Past and Present*, 129 (November 1990), pp. 30–78.

6 Certeau, 'La lecture absolue', pp. 66–7.

7 D. F. McKenzie, *Bibliography and the Sociology of Texts*, The Panizzi Lectures, 1985 (The British Library, London, 1986), p. 20.

8 Carlo Ginzburg, *Il formaggio e i vermi: Il cosmo di un mugnaio del '500* (Einaudi, Turin, 1976), available in English as *The Cheese and the Worms: The Cosmos of a Sixteenth-Century Miller*, tr. John and Anne Tedeschi (Johns Hopkins University Press, Baltimore, 1980); Jean Hébrard, 'Comment Valentin Jamerey-Duval apprit-il à lire? L'autodidaxie exemplaire', in *Pratiques de la lecture*, ed. Roger Chartier (Rivages, Marseilles, 1985), pp. 24–60; *Journal de ma vie, Jacques-Louis Ménétra, compagnon vitrier au XVIIIe siècle*, presented by Daniel Roche (Montalba, Paris, 1982), available in English as Jacques-Louis Ménétra, *Journal of my Life*, with an introduction and commentary by Daniel Roche, tr. Arthur Goldhammer, foreword by Robert Darnton (Columbia University Press, New York, 1986).

9 Roger Chartier, 'Loisir et sociabilité: Lire à haute voix dans l'Europe moderne', *Littératures classiques*, 12 (1990), pp. 127–47, available in English as 'Leisure and Sociability: Reading Aloud in Early Modern Europe', in *Urban Life in the Renaissance*, ed. Susan Zimmerman and Ronald F. E. Weissman (University of Delaware Press, Newark, and

Associated University Press, London and Toronto, 1989), pp. 105–20.

10 Roger E. Stoddard, 'Morphology and the Book From an American Perspective', *Printing History*, 17 (1990), pp. 2–14.

11 For a programmatic definition of *Rezeptionstheorie*, see Hans Robert Jauss, *Literaturgeschichte als Provokation* (Suhrkamp Verlag, Frankfurt, 1974), in French translation as *Pour une esthétique de la réception* (Gallimard, Paris, 1978) and available in English as *Toward an Aesthetic of Reception*, tr. Timothy Bahti, introduction by Paul de Man (University of Minnesota Press, Minneapolis, 1982).

12 D. F. McKenzie, 'Typography and Meaning: The Case of William Congreve', in *Buch und Buchhandel in Europa im achtzehnten Jahrhundert: The Book and the Book Trade in Eighteenth-Century Europe*, Proceedings of the fifth Wolfenbüttler Symposium, 1–3 November 1977, ed. Giles Barber and Bernhard Fabian (Dr Ernst Hauswedell, Hamburg, 1981), pp. 81–126.

13 Henri-Jean Martin with Bruno Delmas, *Histoire et pouvoirs de l'écrit* (Librairie Académique Perrin, Paris, 1988), pp. 295–9, forthcoming in English translation (University of Chicago Press, Chicago).

14 Quoted in McKenzie, *Bibliography and the Sociology of Texts,* pp. 46–7.

15 The essential but debatable work on this topic is Robert Mandrou, *De la culture populaire aux XVIIe et XVIIIe siècles: La Bibliothèque bleue de Troyes* (Stock, Paris, 1964; new ed., Paris: Imago, 1975). For a critique of that work, see Michel de Certeau, Dominique Julia and Jacques Revel, 'La beauté du mort: Le concept de "culture populaire"', *Politique aujourd'hui* (December 1970), pp. 3–23, reprinted in Michel de Certeau, *La culture au pluriel* (1972), 2nd edn (Christian Bourgeois, Paris, 1980), pp. 49–80.

16 Roger Chartier, 'Les livres bleus' and 'Figures littéraires et expériences sociales: La littérature de la gueuserie dans la

Bibliothèque bleue', in his *Lectures et lecteurs dans la France d'Ancien Régime* (Editions du Seuil, Paris, 1987), pp. 247–70, 271–351, respectively, available in English as 'The *Bibliothèque bleue* and Popular Reading' and 'The Literature of Roguery in the *Bibliothèque bleue*', in Chartier, *The Cultural Uses of Print in Early Modern France*, tr. Lydia G. Cochrane (Princeton University Press, Princeton, 1987), pp. 240–64; 265–342.

17 Lawrence W. Levine, 'William Shakespeare and the American People: A Study in Cultural Transformation', *American Historical Review*, 89 (February 1984), pp. 34–66; Levine, *Highbrow/Lowbrow: The Emergence of Cultural Hierarchy in America*, The William E. Massey, Sr Lectures in the History of American Civilization, 1986 (Harvard University Press, Cambridge, Mass. and London, 1988).

18 For a recent reformulation of this question, see David Harlan, 'Intellectual History and the Return of Literature', *American Historical Review*, 94 (June 1989), pp. 581–609.

19 Pierre Bourdieu and Roger Chartier, 'La lecture: Une pratique culturelle', in *Pratiques de la lecture*, ed. Chartier, pp. 217–39.

20 Paul Saenger, 'Silent Reading: Its impact on Late Medieval Script and Society', *Viator, Medieval and Renaissance Studies*, 13 (1982), pp. 367–414; Saenger, 'Physiologie de la lecture et séparation des mots', *Annales E.S.C.* (1989), pp. 939–52.

21 Certeau, *L'invention du quotidien*, pp. 253–4, quoted from Certeau, *The Practice of Everyday Life*, pp. 175–6.

22 Rolf Engelsing, 'Die Perioden der Lesergeschichte in der Neuzeit: Das statistische Ausmass und die soziokulturelle Bedeutung der Lektüre', *Archiv für Geschichte des Buchwesens*, 10 (1970), pp. 945–1002; Erich Schön, *Der Verlust der Sinnlichkeit, oder, Die Verwandlungen des Lesers: Mentalitätswandel um 1800* (Klett-Cotta, Stuttgart, 1987).

23 Philippe Ariès, 'Pour une histoire de la vie privée' and Roger Chartier, 'Les pratiques de l'écrit', in *Histoire de la vie privée*, ed. Philippe Ariès and Georges Duby, 5 vols

(Editions du Seuil, Paris, 1985–7), vol. 3, *De la Renaissance aux Lumières*, ed. Roger Chartier, pp. 7–19 and 112–61, respectively, available in English as Ariès, 'Introduction' and Chartier, 'The Practical Impact of Writing', in *A History of Private Life*, tr. Arthur Goldhammer, 5 vols (Belknap Press of Harvard University Press, Cambridge, Mass. and London, 1987–91), vol. 3, *Passions of the Renaissance*, pp. 1–11 and 111–59.

24 See Robert Darnton, 'First Steps Toward a History of Reading', *Australian Journal of French Studies*, 23, 1 (1986), pp. 5–30.

25 Roger Laufer, 'L'espace visuel du livre ancien', in *Histoire de l'édition française*, ed. Henri-Jean Martin and Roger Chartier, 4 vols (Promodis, Paris, 1982–6), vol. 1, *Le livre conquérant: Du Moyen Age au milieu du XVIIe siècle* (1982), pp. 579–601, reprint edn (Fayard/Cercle de la Librairie, Paris, 1989), pp. 579–601; Laufer, 'Les espaces du livre', in ibid., vol. 2, *Le livre triomphant: 1660–1830* (1984), pp. 128–39, reprint edn (Fayard/Cercle de la Librairie, Paris, 1990), pp. 156–72.

26 See the studies gathered in *Les usages de l'imprimé (XVe–XIXe siècle)*, ed. Roger Chartier (Fayard, Paris, 1987), available in English as Chartier, *The Culture of Print: Power and the Uses of Print in Early Modern Europe*, tr. Lydia G. Cochrane (Princeton University Press, Princeton, 1989).

27 Margaret Spufford, 'First Steps in Literacy: The Reading and Writing Experiences of the Humblest Seventeenth-Century Autobiographers', *Social History*, 4, 3 (1979), pp. 407–35.

28 Giorgio Patrizi, '*Il libro del Cortegiano* e la trattatistica sul comportamento', in *Letteratura italiana*, ed. Alberto Asor Rosa, 8 vols (Einaudi, Turin, 1984), vol. 3, *Le forme del testo*, pt. 2, *La prosa*, pp. 855–90; Roger Chartier, 'Distinction et divulgation: La civilité et ses livres', in Chartier, *Lectures et lecteurs dans la France d'Ancien Régime*, pp. 45–86, available in English as 'From Texts to Manners: A Concept and Its

Books: *Civilité* between Aristocratic Distinction and Popular Appropriation', in Chartier, *The Cultural Uses of Print in Early Modern France*, pp. 71 –109.

29 For examples of this, see Roger Chartier, 'La pendue miraculeusement sauvée: Etude d'un occasionnel', and Catherine Velay-Vallantin, 'Le miroir des contes: Perrault dans les Bibliothèques bleues', in *Les usages de l'imprimé*, ed. Chartier, pp. 83–127 and 129–55, respectively, available in English as 'The Hanged Woman Miraculously Saved: An *occasionnel*' and 'Tales as a Mirror: Perrault in the *Bibliothèque bleue*', in *The Culture of Print*, ed. Chartier, pp. 59–91 and 92–136, respectively.

30 Certeau, *L'invention du quotidien*, p. 249, quoted from *The Practice of Everyday Life*, p. 172.

31 Stanley Fish, *Is There a Text in This Class? The Authority of Interpretive Communities* (Harvard University Press, Cambridge, Mass. and London, 1980).

Chapter 2   Figures of the Author

1 D. F. McKenzie, *Bibliography and the Sociology of Texts*, The Panizzi Lectures 1985 (The British Library, London, 1986), p. 7.

2 G. Thomas Tanselle, 'Analytical Bibliography and Renaissance Printing History', *Printing History*, 3, 1 (1981), pp. 24–33.

3 For an overview of the history of the book in France, see Roger Chartier, *Frenchness in the History of the Book: From the History of Publishing to the History of Reading*, The 1987 James Russell Wiggins Lecture, Worcester, Mass., American Antiquarian Society, 1988, published in French as 'De l'histoire du livre à l'histoire de la lecture', *Archives et Bibliothèques de Belgique/Archief- en Bibliotheekwezen in België*, 10, 1–2 (1989), pp. 161–89.

4 Lucien Febvre and Henri-Jean Martin, *L'apparition du livre* (1958), new ed., L'Evolution de l'Humanité (Albin Michel,

Paris, 1971), p. 14, quoted from *The Coming of the Book: The Impact of Printing 1450–1800*, ed. Geoffrey Nowell-Smith and David Wootton, tr. David Gerard (Verso, London, 1984), p. 11.

5 Out of an immense bibliography, let me recall only the founding text: Hans Robert Jauss, *Literaturgeschichte als Provokation* (Suhrkamp Verlag, Frankfurt, 1974), in French translation as *Pour une esthétique de la réception* (Gallimard, Paris, 1978) and available in English as *Toward an Aesthetic of Reception*, tr. Timothy Bahti (University of Minnesota Press, Minneapolis, 1982).

6 For one example, see Stephen Jay Greenblatt, *Shakespearean Negotiations: The Circulation of Social Energy in Renaissance England* (University of California Press, Berkeley, 1988). For an overview, see *The New Historicism* ed. H. Aram Veeser (Routledge, New York and London, 1989), esp. Stephen Jay Greenblatt, 'Towards a Poetics of Culture', pp. 1–14, which includes the phrase: 'The work of art is the product of a negotiation between a creator or a class of creators, and the institutions and practices of society.'

7 For one example, see Alain Viala, *La Naissance de l'écrivain: Sociologie de la littérature à l'âge classique* (Editions de Minuit, Paris, 1985). The theoretical basis of this approach is given in the founding texts of Pierre Bourdieu, in particular, 'Champ intellectuel et projet créateur', *Les Temps Modernes*, 246 (November 1966), pp. 865–906; Bourdieu, 'Structuralism and Theory of Sociological Knowledge', *Social Research*, 35, 4 (winter 1968), pp. 681–706; and the recent Bourdieu, *Les règles de l'art: Genèse et structure du champ littéraire* (Editions du Seuil, Paris, 1992).

8 McKenzie, *Bibliography and the Sociology of Texts*, esp. 'The Book as an Expressive Form', pp. 1–21.

9 Michel Foucault, 'Qu'est-ce qu'un auteur?' *Bulletin de la Société française de Philosophie*, 44 (July–September 1969), pp. 73–104, reprinted in *Littoral*, 9 (1983), pp. 3–32, available in English as 'What Is an Author?' in Michel

Foucault, *Language, Counter-Memory, Practice: Selected Essays and Interviews*, ed. and introduction by Donald F. Bouchard (Cornell University Press, Ithaca, NY, 1977), pp. 113–138, and quoted here from Foucault, 'What is an Author?' in *Textual Strategies: Perspectives in Post-Structural Criticism*, ed. Josué V. Harari (Cornell University Press, Ithaca, N.Y., 1979), pp. 141–60, quotations pp. 141, 148, 153, 144, 148, 149.

10 Among the most important recent works are Martha Woodmansee, 'The Genius and the Copyright: Economic and Legal Conditions of the Emergence of the "Author"', *Eighteenth-Century Studies*, 17, 4 (1984), pp. 425–48; Mark Rose, 'The Author as Proprietor: *Donaldson v. Becket* and the Genealogy of Modern Authorship', *Representations*, 23 (1988), pp. 51–85; Carla Hesse, 'Enlightenment Epistemology and the Laws of Authorship in Revolutionary France, 1777–1793', *Representations*, 30 (1990), pp. 109–37.

11 Denis Diderot, *Sur la liberté de la presse*, partial text established, presented, and annotated by Jacques Proust (Editions Sociales, Paris, 1964). On Diderot's text, see Roger Chartier, *Les origines culturelles de la Révolution française* (Editions du Seuil, Paris, 1990), pp. 69–80, available in English as Chartier, *The Cultural Origins of the French Revolution*, tr. Lydia G. Cochrane (Duke University Press, Durham N.C. and London, 1991), pp. 53–61.

12 Rose, 'The Author as Proprietor', p. 56.

13 Cited in Raymond Birn, 'The Profits of Ideas: *Privilèges en librairie* in Eighteenth-Century France', *Eighteenth-Century Studies*, 4, 2 (1971), pp. 131–68, quotation (in French) p. 161.

14 William Enfield, *Observations on Literary Property* (London: 1774), quoted from Rose, 'The Author as Proprietor', p. 59.

15 Baron James Eyre in *Cases of the Appellants and Respondents in the Cause of Literary Property Before the House of Lords* (London: 1774), p. 34, quoted from Rose, 'The Author as Proprietor', p. 61.

16 See the analysis in Carla Hesse, 'Enlightenment Epistemology and the Laws of Authorship'. Hesse emphasizes the impact of Condorcet's and Sieyès's position on revolutionary legislation: 'The democratic bourgeois revolution did not mark a further step in the progressive consolidation of the notion of the author. Rather, the revolutionaries explicitly intended to dethrone the absolute author, a creature of privilege, and recast him, not as a *private* individual (the absolute bourgeois), but rather as a *public* servant, as the model citizen' (p. 130).

17 See Woodmansee, 'The Genius and the Copyright', esp. her analysis (pp. 444–6) of the distinction between form and content as proposed by Fichte in his essay, 'Beweis der Unrechtmässigkeit des Büchernachdrucks: Ein Räsonnement und eine Parabel' (1793).

18 Roland Mortier, *L'originalité: Une nouvelle catégorie esthétique au siècle des Lumières* (Droz, Geneva, 1982).

19 Martha Woodmansee, 'The Interests in Disinterestedness: Karl Philip Moritz and the Emergence of the Theory of Aesthetic Autonomy in Eighteenth-Century Germany', *Modern Language Quarterly*, 45 (1984), pp. 22–47.

20 On the evolution of this change, see Eric Walter, 'Les auteurs et le champ littéraire', in *Histoire de l'édition française*, ed. Henri-Jean Martin and Roger Chartier, 4 vols (Promodis, Paris, 1982–6), vol. 2, *Le livre triomphant, 1660–1830*, pp. 382–99, reprint edn (Fayard/Cercle de la Librairie, Paris 1990), pp. 499–518; Siegfried Jüttner, 'The Status of Writer', in *Seventh International Congress on the Enlightenment: Introductory Papers / Septième congrès international des Lumières: rapports préliminaires*, Budapest 26 July – 2 August 1987 (The Voltaire Foundation, Oxford, 1987), pp. 173–201.

21 Lord Camden in *Cases of the Appellants and Respondents in the Cause of Literary Property Before the House of Lords* (London 1774), p. 54, quoted in Rose, 'The Author as Proprietor', p. 68.

22 Viala, *La Naissance de l'écrivain*, pp. 51–84.

23 Alvin Kernan, *Printing Technology, Letters & Samuel Johnson* (Princeton University Press, Princeton, 1987), quotations pp. 88, 47, 42, 64, 65, 22, 23. On the circulation of works in manuscript, see Harold Love, 'Scribal Publication in Seventeenth-Century England', *Transactions of the Cambridge Bibliographical Society*, vol. 9, pt 2 (1987), pp. 130–54.

24 I might note that the *Dictionnaire de l'Académie Française* (1694) does not establish as explicit a connection between author and printing as this, indicating only, '*Auteur*, Is said particularly of One who has composed a book.'

25 On the particular status of the woman author from the viewpoint of her juridical inferiority, see Carla Hesse, 'Reading Signatures: Female Authorship and Revolutionary Laws in France, 1750–1850', *Eighteenth-Century Studies*, 22, 3 (1989), pp. 469–87.

26 *Premier Volume de la Bibliothèque du Sieur de La Croix du Maine* (Abel L'Angelier, Paris, 1584); *La Bibliothèque d'Antoine du Verdier, seigneur de Vauprivas* (Barthélémy Honorat, Lyons, 1585). The two works were republished together in the eighteenth century under the title, *Les Bibliothèques Françaises de La Croix du Maine et de Du Verdier, sieur de Vauprivas*, Nouvelle Edition dédiée au Roi, revue, corrigée et augmentée d'un discours sur le Progrès des Lettres en France, et des Remarques historiques, critiques et littéraires de M. de la Monnoye et de M. le Président Bouhier, de l'Académie française, de M. Falconet, de l'Académie des Belles-Lettres, par M. Rigoley de Juvigny, 6 vols (Saillant et Nyon et Michel Lambert, Paris, 1772–3).

27 La Croix du Maine gives the source of this evaluation as 'La *Librairie* d'Antoine François Dony, Florentin', which is Anton Francesco Doni, *La Libraria del Doni, Fiorentino, Nella quale sono scritti tutti gl'autori vulgari con cento discorsi sopra quelli* (Gabriele Giolito de' Ferrari, Venice, 1550) and republished under the title *La Libraria del Doni, Fiorentino, divisa in tre trattati. Nel primo sono scritti, tutti gl'*

autori volgari con cento e piu discorsi, sopra di quelli. Nel secondo sono dati in luce tutti i libri che l'autore ha veduti a penna, il nome de' componitori, dell'opere, i titoli, e le materie. Nel terzo, si legge l'inventione dell'Academie, insieme con i sopranomi, i motti, le imprese, et l'opere fatte da tutti gli Academici (Gabriele Giolito de' Ferrari, Venice, 1557). It is worth noting that unlike the *Bibliothèques* of La Croix du Maine and Du Verdier, which were published in monumental folio editions, the works of Anton Francesco Doni were easy to handle and to carry since they were printed in smaller formats, duodecimo for the 1550 edition and octavo in 1557. On Doni's *Libraria*, see Amedeo Quondam, 'La letteratura in tipografia', in *Letteratura italiana*, ed. Alberto Asor Rosa, 8 vols (Giulio Einaudi, Turin, 1982–91), vol. 2, *Produzione e consumo*, pp. 555–686, esp. 620–36.

28 On title pages in the sixteenth and seventeenth centuries, see Roger Laufer, 'L'espace visuel du livre ancien', in *Histoire de l'édition française*, vol. 1, *Le livre conquérant: Du Moyen Age au milieu du XVIIe siècle* (1982), pp. 478–97, reprint edn (Fayard/Cercle de la Librairie, 1989), pp. 579–601.

29 This title page is reproduced in Miguel de Cervantes, *El Ingenioso Hidalgo Don Quijote de la Mancha*, ed. John Jay Allen, 2 vols (Cátedra, Madrid, 1984), 1:43.

30 Cervantes, *El Ingenioso Hidalgo Don Quijote de la Mancha*, p. 67, quoted from *The Adventures of Don Quixote de la Mancha*, tr. J. M. Cohen (Penguin Books, Harmondsworth, 1950), p. 25.

31 Ibid., pp. 143–9, *The Adventures of Don Quixote*, p. 77.

32 Joseph Loewenstein, 'The Script in the Marketplace', *Representations*, 12 (1985), pp. 101–14, quotation p. 109.

33 Annie Parent, *Les métiers du livre à Paris au XVIe siècle (1535–1560)* (Librairie Droz, Geneva, 1974), pp. 98–121, 286–311, quotation p. 301. Parent presents twenty-three contracts between authors and printers or

booksellers in Paris. On *privilèges*, see Elizabeth Armstrong, *Before Copyright: The French Book-Privilege System, 1498–1526* (Cambridge University Press, Cambridge, 1990).

34 Robert Darnton, 'A Police Inspector Sorts His Files: The Anatomy of the Republic of Letters', in Darnton, *The Great Cat Massacre and Other Episodes in French Cultural History* (Basic Books, New York, 1984), pp. 144–89, and Darnton, 'The Facts of Literary Life in Eighteenth-Century France', in *The Political Culture of the Old Regime*, ed. Keith Michael Baker (Pergamon Press, Oxford, 1987), pp. 261–91.

35 Foucault's essay has been read in two ways. One way stresses the connection between the author-function and the philosophical and juridical definition of the individual and of private property (see Hesse, 'Enlightenment Epistemology and the Laws of Authorship', p. 109: 'The relation between the "author" and the "text," [Foucault] suggests, emerged historically as the cultural incarnation of a new axis in sociopolitical discourse: the inviolable relation between the rights-bearing individual and private property'). The other way emphasizes the dependence of the author-function on state and church censorship (as with Joseph Loewenstein, who recognizes, speaking of Foucault in 'The Script in the Marketplace', p. 111, 'His nearly exclusive concentration of the effect of the censoriousness of Church and State on the development of modern authorship has been salutary, though it slights the effect of the *market* in books on that development'). The first reading leads to emphasizing the eighteenth century; the second, the sixteenth century.

36 J. M. De Bujanda, Francis M. Higman, James K. Farge, *L'Index de l'Université de Paris, 1544, 1545, 1547, 1551, 1556* (Editions de l'Université de Sherbrooke, Sherbrooke; Librairie Droz, Geneva, 1985), which reproduces the various catalogues of the books censured by the Sorbonne. See

also James K. Farge, *Orthodoxy and Reform in Early Reformation France: The Faculty of Theology of Paris, 1500–1543* (E. J. Brill, Leiden, 1985), pp. 213–19. The decisive role of inquisitorial indexes in the affirmation of the author-function is implicitly recognized for Spain in Eugenio Asensio, 'Fray Luis de Maluenda, apologista de la Inquisición, condemnado en el Indice Inquisitorial', *Arquivos do Centro Cultural Português* (1975), pp. 87–100, quoted from Francisco Rico, 'Introducción', *Lazarillo de Tormes* (Cátedra, Madrid, 1987), pp. 32–3: '*Before* [emphasis mine] the Catalogue of the books of 1559 ... decreed strict dispositions against anonymous impressions, anonymity was the rule for books of entertainment and piety in Castilian. *La Celestina* and many of its imitations was published anonymously, as were many chivalric romances, *Lazarillo* and its sequel, and, finally, a fairly large number of books of devotion in the form of romances.'

37 Jeanne Veyrin-Forrer, 'Antoine Augereau, graveur de lettres, imprimeur et libraire parisien (d.1534)', *Paris et Ile-de-France: Mémoires publiés par la Fédération des Sociétés historiques et archéologiques de Paris et de l'Ile-de-France*, 8 (1956), pp. 103–56, reprinted in Veyrin-Forrer, *La lettre et le texte: Trente années de recherches sur l'histoire du livre* (Collection de l'Ecole Normale Supérieure de Jeunes Filles, Paris, 1987), pp. 3–50.

38 On the trial of Etienne Dolet in 1543, see Francis Higman, *Censorship and the Sorbonne: A Bibliographical Study of Books in French Censored by the Faculty of Theology of the University of Paris, 1520–1551* (Librairie Droz, Geneva, 1979), pp. 96–9.

39 On the 'Dolet case', the classic article is Lucien Febvre, 'Dolet, propagateur de l'Evangile', *Bibliothèque d'Humanisme et Renaissance*, 7 (1945), pp. 98–170, reprinted in Febvre, *Au coeur religieux du XVIe siècle*, 2nd edn (S.E.V.P.E.N., Paris, 1968), pp. 172–224, reprint edn. (Paris: LGF, livre de poche, 1984); *Etienne Dolet*

(1509–1546), Cahiers V.-L. Saulnier, 3 (Collection de l'Ecole Normale Supérieure de Jeunes Filles, Paris, 1986).

40 Ruth Mortimer, *A Portrait of the Author in Sixteenth-Century France: A Paper* (Hanes Foundation, Rare Book Collection, Academic Affairs Library, University of North Carolina at Chapel Hill, Chapel Hill, 1980).

41 For a first corpus of representations of the author in miniatures in manuscripts, see the references in Paul Saenger, 'Silent Reading: Its Impact on Late Medieval Script and Society', *Viator, Medieval and Renaissance Studies*, 13 (1982), pp. 367–414, esp. 388–90, 407.

42 On the 1710 edition of Congreve's *Works*, see D. F. McKenzie, 'When Congreve Made a Scene', *Transactions of the Cambridge Bibliographical Society*, 7, 3 (1979), pp. 338–42; McKenzie, 'Typography and Meaning: The Case of William Congreve', in *Buch und Buchhandel in Europa im achtzehnten Jahrhundert: The Book and the Book Trade in Eighteenth-Century Europe*, ed. Giles Barber and Bernhard Fabian (Dr Ernst Hauswedell, Hamburg, 1981), pp. 81–126. For an overview of Congreve's relations with print culture, see Julie Stone Peters, *Congreve, the Drama, and the Printed Word* (Stanford University Press, Stanford, Cal., 1990).

43 Annie Parent, *Les métiers du livre*, pp. 291, 297, 307, and 305. See also Parent, 'Ambroise Paré et ses "imprimeurs-libraires"', *Actes du Colloque International 'Ambroise Paré et son temps'*, 24–5 November, Laval (Mayenne) (Association de commémoration du Quadricentennaire de la mort d'Ambroise Paré, Laval, n.d.), pp. 207–33.

44 Armando Petrucci, 'Il libro manoscritto', in *Letteratura italiana*, ed. Asor Rosa, vol. 2, pp. 499–524, esp. 516–17. For an example of control exercised by the author over the copyist of his works, see Peter J. Lucas, 'John Capgrave O.S.A. (1395–1464): Scribe and "Publischer"', *Transactions of the Cambridge Bibliographical Society*, 5, 1 (1969), pp. 1–35.

45 Petrucci, 'Il libro manoscritto', pp. 512–3, 520–2.

46 Jacqueline Cerquiglini, 'Quand la voix s'est tue: La mise en recueil de la poésie lyrique aux XIVe et XVe siècles', in *Der Ursprung von Literatur: Medien, Rollen,Kommunikationssituationen zwischen 1450 und 1650*, ed. Gisela Smolka-Koerdt, Peter M. Spangenberg, Dagmar Tillmann-Bartylla (Wilhelm Fink Verlag, Munich, 1988), pp. 136–48.

47 Gemma Guerrini, 'Il sistema di communicazione di un "corpus" di manoscritti quattrocenteschi: I "Trionfi" del Petrarca', *Scrittura e civiltà*, 10 (1986), pp. 122–97.

48 Maurice Laugaa, *La pensée du pseudonyme* (Presses Universitaires de France, Paris, 1986), esp. his analysis (pp. 195–221, 255–78) of Adrien Baillet, *Auteurs déguisez sous des noms étrangers: Empruntez, Supposez, Feints à plaisir: Chiffrez, Renversez, Retournez, ou Changez d'une langue en une autre* (Antoine Dezallier, Paris, 1690). For an example of a complaint against the usurpations of identity, see the *Memorial* of Lope de Vega directed at the authors of 'Relaciones, Coplas, y otros géneros de versos' who 'print and have it cried in the streets that the text was composed by Alonso de Ledesma, Niñan de Riaza, Baltasar de Medinilla, Lope de Vega and other persons known for their books and studies in this same genre, to the price of great harm done to their reputation and even to their life by the printing of satires against the cities and against the persons that are known by their titles, their charges, and their noble deeds': text published and analysed in María Cruz García de Enterría, *Sociedad y poesia de cordel en el barroco* (Taurus, Madrid, 1973), pp. 85–130.

49 Steven Shapin, 'The House of Experiment in Seventeenth-Century England', *Isis*, 79 (1988), pp. 373–404.

50 On the writing strategies implied by the existence of a censorship of print production, see Annabel M. Patterson, *Censorship and Interpretation: The Conditions of Writing and Reading in Early Modern England* (University of Wisconsin Press, Madison, Wis., 1984), esp. the chapter entitled

'Prynne's Ears; or, The Hermeneutics of Censorship', pp. 44–119.

Chapter 3   Libraries without Walls

1 Jorge Luis Borges, 'The Library of Babel', in Borges, *Labyrinths: Selected Stories and Other Writings*, ed. Donald A. Yates and James E. Irby (New Directions, New York, 1964), pp. 54–5.

2 On Boullée's design, see Jean-Marie Pérouse de Montclos, *Etienne-Louis Boullée (1728–1799): De l'architecture classique à l'architecture révolutionnaire* (Arts et Métiers Graphiques, Paris, 1969), pp. 166–7 and plates 96–102.

3 Gabriel Naudé, *Advis pour dresser une bibliothèque*, reproduction of the 1644 edition, preceded by Claude Jolly, 'L'*Advis*, manifeste de la bibliothèque érudite' (Aux Amateurs de Livres, Paris 1990). On Naudé's text, see Jean Viardot, 'Livres rares et pratiques bibliophiliques', in *Histoire de l'édition française*, ed. Henri-Jean Martin and Roger Chartier, 4 vols (Promodis, Paris, 1982–6), vol. 2, *Le livre triomphant: 1660–1830*, pp. 446–67, esp. pp. 448–50, reprint edn (Fayard/Cercle de la Librairie, Paris, 1900), pp. 593–614; Viardot, 'Naissance de la bibliophilie: Les cabinets de livres rares', in *Histoire des bibliothèques françaises*, 3 vols (Promodis/Cercle de la Librairie, Paris, 1988–91), vol. 2, *Les bibliothèques sous l'Ancien Régime*, 1530–1789), ed. Claude Jolly, pp. 269–89, esp. 270–1.

4 Naudé, *Advis*, p. 104.

5 Ibid., p. 12.

6 Ibid., p. 31.

7 Ibid., p. 37.

8 Ibid., p. 57.

9 Jean Sgard, ed., *Dictionnaire des journaux 1600–1789* (Universitas, Paris, 1991), items nos 144–74.

10 Roger Poirier, *La Bibliothèque universelle des romans: Rédacteurs, textes, publics* (Librairie Droz, Geneva, 1977).

11 Louis-Sébastien Mercier, *Tableau de Paris, Nouvelle édition revue et augmentée*, 12 vols (Amsterdam, 1782–3), vol. 6, *Dictionnaires*, pp. 294–5.

12 For example, see Hans-Jürgen Lüsebrink, 'L' "Histoire des Deux Indes" et ses "extraits": Un mode de dispersion textuelle au XVIIIe siècle', *Littérature*, 69, 'Intertextualité et Révolution' (February 1988), pp. 28–41.

13 Louis-Sébastien Mercier, *L'An 2440: Rêve s'il en fut jamais*, ed., introduction and notes by Raymond Trousson (Editions Ducros, Bordeaux, 1971), chap. 28, 'La bibliothèque du roi', pp. 247–71, quotations pp. 247–8, 250–1.

14 Jean Marie Goulemot, 'En guise de conclusion: Les bibliothèques imaginaires (fictions romanesques et utopies)', in *Histoire des bibliothèques françaises*, 2:500–11.

15 Furetière was alluding not only to the *Bibliotheca universalis* of Gesner but also to Antonio Possevino, S.J., *Bibliotheca selecta qua agitur de ratione studiorum* (Ex Typographia Apostolica Vaticana, Roma, 1593; Venice, 1603; Cologne 1607); Photius, *Myriobiblion sive Bibliotheca librorum quos legit et censuit Photius . . . Graece edidit David Hoeschelius . . . et notis illustravit, latine vero reddidit et scholiis auxit Andreas Schottus* (Rouen, 1653, after the Greek and Latin editions published in Augsburg in 1601 and 1606); Philippe Labbé, S.J., *Bibliotheca bibliothecarum curis secundis auctior* (L. Billaine, Paris, 1664; Rouen, 1672).

16 Naudé, *Advis*, pp. 22, 24.

17 The two Spanish 'libraries' that Furetière mentions are Nicolás Antonio, *Bibliotheca hispana, sive Hispanorum qui . . . scripto aliquid consignaverunt notitia* (Rome, 1672; 1696) and Andreas Schott or Andreas Schott Peregrinus, S.J., *Hispaniae bibliotheca, seu de academiciis ac bibliothecis; item elogia et nomenclator clarorum Hispaniae scriptorum* (Frankfurt, 1608).

18 Theodore Besterman, *The Beginnings of Systematic Bibliography* (Oxford University Press, Oxford; Humphrey Milford, London, 1935); Luigi Balsamo, *La bibliografia: Storia*

di una tradizione (Sansoni, Florence, 1984), available in English as *Bibliography: History of a Tradition*, tr. William A. Pettas (B. M. Rosenthal, Berkeley, 1990). Helmut Zedelmaier, *Bibliotheca Universalis und Bibliotheca Selecta: Das Problem der Ordnung das gelehrten Wissens in der frühen Neuzeit* (Böhlau Verlag, Cologne, Weimar, Vienna, 1992) was published after this essay was written.

19 There is an abundant bibliography on Gesner as a bibliographer: see Jens Christian Bay, 'Conrad Gesner (1516–1565): The Father of Bibliography: An Appreciation', *Papers of the Bibliographical Society of America*, 10 (1916), pp. 53–88, published separately as *Conrad Gesner, The Father of Bibliography: An Appreciation* (Chicago, 1916); Paul-Emile Schazmann, 'Conrad Gesner et les débuts de la bibliographie universelle', *Libri* (1952/3), pp. 37–49; Josef Mayerhöfer, 'Conrad Gessner als Bibliograph und Enzyklopädist', *Gesnerus*, 3/4 (1965), pp. 176–94; Hans Widman, 'Nachtwort', in Konrad Gesner, *Bibliotheca universalis und Appendix* (Otto Zeller Verlagsbuchhandlung, Osnabrück, 1966), pp. i–xii; Hans Fischer, 'Conrad Gesner (1516–1565) as Bibliographer and Encyclopedist', *The Library*, 5th ser. 21, 4 (December 1966), pp. 269–81; Hans H. Wellisch, 'Conrad Gesner: A Bio-Bibliography', *Journal of the Society for the Bibliography of Natural History* (1975), pp. 151–247, 2nd edn revised pubished under the same title (IDC, Zug, 1984); Luigi Balsamo, 'Il canone bibliografico di Konrad Gesner e il concetto di biblioteca pubblica nel Cinquecento', in *Studi di biblioteconomia e storia del libro in onore di Francesco Barberi* (Associazione italiana biblioteche, Rome, 1976), 77–96; Josef Hejnic and Václav Bok, *Gesner europäische Bibliographie und ihre Beziehung zum Späthumanismus in Böhmen und Mähren* (Academia Nakladetelství Cekoslovenské, Akademie Ved, Prague, 1988); Alfredo Serrai, *Conrad Gesner*, ed. Maria Cochetti, with a bibliography of Gesner's works by Marco Menato (Bulzoni, Rome, 1990).

20 For a reprint of this text, see Anton Francesco Doni, *La libraria*, ed. Vanni Bramanti (Longanesi, Milan, 1972). See also Cecilia Ricottini Marsili-Libelli, *Anton Francesco Doni, scrittore e stampatore* (Sansoni Antiquariato, Florence, 1960); Amedeo Quondam, 'La letteratura in tipografia', in *Letteratura italiana*, ed. Alberto Asor Rosa, 8 vols (Giulio Einaudi, Turin, 1983), vol. 2, *Produzione e consumo*, pp. 555–686, esp. 620–36.

21 Quondam, 'La letteratura in tipografia', pp. 628–9.

22 Besterman, *The Beginnings of Systematic Bibliography*, p. 23.

23 I shall quote from Du Verdier's and La Croix du Maine's works from the copies in the Bibliothèque Nationale de Paris. On these two *Bibliothèques*, see Claude Longeon, 'Antoine Du Verdier et François de La Croix du Maine', *Actes du Colloque Renaissance–Classicisme du Maine*, Le Mans, May 1971 (A.-G. Nizet, Paris, 1975), pp. 213–33.

24 Armando Petrucci, 'Alle origini del libro moderno: Libri da banco, libro da bisaccia, libretti da mano', in *Libri, scrittura e pubblico nel Rinascimento: Guida storica e critica*, ed. Armando Petrucci (Laterza, Rome and Bari, 1979), pp. 137–56.

25 On the history of classification, see the very dogmatic E. I. Samurin, *Geschichte der bibliothekarisch–bibliographischen Klassifikation*, originally published in Russian (Moscow, 1955) (VEB Bibliographisches Institut, Leipzig, 1964), on La Croix du Maine, Band I, pp. 106–109 (also available, 2 vols in 1, Verlag Dokumentation, Munich, 1977). See also Henri-Jean Martin, 'Classements et conjonctures', in *Histoire de l'édition française*, ed. Martin and Chartier, vol. 1, *Le livre conquérant: Du Moyen Age au milieu du XVIIe siècle*, pp. 429–41, reprint edn (Fayard/Cercle de la Librairie, Paris, 1989), pp. 529–62.

26 Quondam, 'La letteratura in tipografia', p. 623.

27 Michel Foucault, 'Qu'est-ce qu'un auteur?' *Bulletin de la Société française de Philosophie*, 44 (July–September 1969), pp. 73–104, reprinted in *Littoral*, 9 (1983), pp. 3–32, available in English as 'What Is an Author?' in *Textual*

Strategies: Perspectives in Post-Structural Criticism, ed. Josué V. Harari (Cornell University Press, Ithaca, N.Y., 1979), pp. 141–60.

28 Claude Longeon, 'Antoine du Verdier (11 novembre 1544–25 septembre 1600)', in Longeon, *Les écrivains foréziens du XVIe siècle: Répertoire bio-bibliographique* (Centre d'Etudes Foréziennes, Saint-Etienne, 1970), pp. 288–316.

29 J. M. De Bujanda, Francis M. Higman, James K. Farge, *L'Index de l'Université de Paris, 1544, 1545, 1547, 1551, 1556* (Editions de l'Université de Sherbrooke, Sherbrooke; Librairie Droz, Geneva, 1985). On the utilization of given names and 'surnames' (which became family names), see Anne Lefebvre-Teillard, *Le Nom: Droit et histoire* (Presses Universitaires de France, Paris, 1990).

Epilogue

1 D. F. McKenzie, *Bibliography and the Sociology of Texts*, The Panizzi Lectures 1985 (The British Library, London, 1986), p. 4.

2 Roger E. Stoddard, *Marks in Books Illustrated and Explained* (The Houghton Library, Harvard University, Cambridge, Mass., 1985). As examples of studies that take hand-written entries presented in printed works as a fundamental source of a history of reading and interpretation, see Cathy N. Davidson, *Revolution and the Word: The Rise of the Novel in America* (Oxford University Press, Oxford and New York, 1986), pp. 75–9; Lisa Jardine and Anthony Grafton, '"Studied for Action": How Gabriel Harvey Read His Livy', *Past and Present*, 129 (November 1990), pp. 30–78.

3 The fundamental work on the various definitions of the metaphor of the book in the Western philosophical tradition is Hans Blumenberg, *Die Lesbarkeit der Welt* (Suhrkamp, Frankfurt, 1981, 2nd edn 1983), also available in Italian translation as *La leggibilità del mondo: Il libro come metafora della natura* (Il Mulino, Bologna, 1984).

4 On the difficult and controversial question of the shift from the *volumen* to the *codex*, see Colin H. Roberts and T. C. Skeat, *The Birth of the Codex* (Published for the British Academy by the Oxford University Press, London and New York, 1983, 1987); *Les débuts du codex*, ed. Alain Blanchard, Actes de la Journée d'Etudes organisée à Paris par l'Institut de Papyrologie de la Sorbonne et l'Institut de recherche et d'histoire des textes, les 3 et 4 juillet 1985 (Brepols, Turnhout, 1989); and the revision proposed in Guglielmo Cavallo, 'Testo, Libro, Lettura', in *Lo spazio letterario di Roma antica*, ed. Guglielmo Cavallo, Paolo Fedeli, and Andrea Giardina, 5 vols (Salerno Editrice, Rome, 1989), vol. 2, *La circolazione del testo*, pp. 307–41; Cavallo, 'Libro e cultura scritta', in *Storia di Roma*, ed. Arnaldo Momigliano and Aldo Schiavone, 4 vols (Einaudi, Turin, 1988–), vol. 4, *Caratteri e morfologie*, pp. 693–734.

Index